Composition

Roby
Watson

WONDERS OF NATURE

**A CHILD'S INTRODUCTION
TO THE WORLD OF ANIMALS, PLANTS,
BIRDS, FISH & INSECTS**

Published By
PARENTS' MAGAZINE PRESS

A division of
Parents' Magazine Enterprises, Inc.
New York, N.Y.

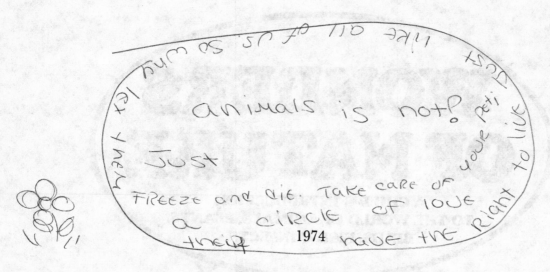

1974

Parents' Magazine Enterprises, Inc.

For

PLAYMORE, INC.

New York, New York

From: Children's Guide To Knowledge (Chap. 1-8)
Copyright MCMLXIII, Parents' Magazine Enterprises, Inc.
Library of Congress Catalog Card No. 63-11929

"INTRODUCTION about this Book"

Robyn
Elizabeth
Watson!

"eighty one is the Best"

This single over-sized volume introduces children to the fabulous *Wonders of Nature* — the world not made by man. It acquaints children in simple text and colorful illustrations with the fascinating world of animals, both wild and domestic; with fish and reptiles; flowers and plants; trees and shrubs; birds, butterflies, bees, bugs and other insects.

Among the aims of this volume is the hope of inducing a greater interest in the wondrous forms of nature, as well as in the fun of reading. Thus, every page has been beautifully illustrated with original drawings, many in full color. These paintings with the accompanying text have been designed to so arouse the curiosity of the young child that he will go on to other books and sources of information and, thus, further broaden his knowledge of the world around him.

The Editors

CONTENTS

BUTTERFLIES, BEES, BUGS AND OTHER INSECTS

FISH, SHELLFISH, AND REPTILES

FLOWERS AND PLANTS

TREES AND SHRUBS

Pets

Terriers
Long-Legged Terriers
Short-Legged Terriers
Beagles
Greyhounds
Spaniels
Boxers
St. Bernards
Collies
German Shepherds
Police Dogs
Setters
Dachshunds
Chihuahuas
Bulldogs and Mastiffs
Boston Terriers
Pekingese
Poodles
Great Danes
Doberman Pinschers
Dalmatians
Eskimo Dogs
Pomeranians
Tabby Cats
Persians
Maine
Siamese
Burmese
Maltese
Abyssinians
Manx
Bird Pets
Talking Birds
Singing Birds
Fishes
Caged Pets
Hamsters
Guinea Pigs
White Mice
Rabbits

THE first animals men knew were the wild ones they caught to eat. But while they were hunting for their food, another wild animal that hunted along with them became their closest friend. This was the wild dog.

The wild dogs were faster than men, and could see farther and smell farther, so their help was welcome. But men had learned to make arrows and spears and stone knives to kill the food animals, and when it came time to eat men built a fire. The dogs curled up by the fire, and shared the food they had helped to catch. By these

4

forest fireplaces dogs and men became friends.

Dogs were the first pets. Pets are special kinds of tame animals that are kept not because they are useful, for food or their wool or skins, or because they help in farm work, but because they are fun to have around. Of course many pets are helpful to their owners. Dogs herd sheep and cattle, help the police, and guide the blind. Cats catch mice. But dogs and cats are also wonderful companions. Later, people found that even mice and birds and fish and rabbits were fun. So all these became pets.

tabby

"Playful little kitten"

English setter!

"Joining a tea party"

AIREDALE

"good" "house" dogs!

TERRIERS

THERE are several different breeds of Terrier. They were originally called "earth dogs" (that is what Terrier means), and were used to catch small animals.

Now Terriers are mostly housedogs, and they make fine guardians, because they bark fiercely if an unwelcome stranger comes near. There are long-legged and short-legged kinds.

LONG-LEGGED TERRIERS

THE Airedale is a long-legged Terrier about two feet high and usually colored tan. Bull Terriers, usually white, are the strongest dogs for their weight, and yet they are noted for their gentleness. One dog of this kind, finding it had to fight a tiny Pekingese which teased it, picked the little fellow up and placed it gently in a waste basket.

"sweet" dogs!

Fox Terriers, both smooth and wire-haired, are gay, brave, loyal, and lovely to look at. Other long-legged Terriers are the Irish, the Welsh, and the Bedlington.

SCOTTIE

WIREHAIRED
TERRIER

SHORT-LEGGED TERRIERS

THE best known short-legged Terriers are the Scotties. They are shaggy. often black or sand-colored, with small pointed ears and erect tails. Sealyham and Dandie Dinmonts are other short-legged Terriers.

Many Terriers have lived in the White House, among them Theodore Roosevelt's Scamp, Woodrow Wilson's Davie, Calvin Coolidge's Peter Pan, and Franklin D. Roosevelt's Fala.

FOX TERRIER

BEAGLES

THE Beagle is a merry dog, about a foot high, with a short coat of no special color—it can be black-and-white, tan, or a combination. The Beagle is really a kind of hound, and its notion of a good time is to chase rabbits across a rough field.

No dog is more gentle and affectionate than the Beagle, especially if it is treated with kindness. But the kindest thing you can do is to be sure it gets out for a good run ever so often!

"Good Pets" And Good hunters!

"Racing" dogs!

GREYHOUNDS

GREYHOUNDS are swift dogs with long, narrow heads. They are not always grey, in spite of their name. They were used for hunting as long as 6,000 years ago. Now they are used as pets and in dog racing.

SPANIELS

SPANIELS get their name from Spain, where they were bred 700 years ago. Spaniels enjoy retrieving because they are really hunting dogs, long trained to find and bring back birds that hunters have shot. Some Spaniels like water so much that they are called Water Spaniels. Cocker Spaniels have their name because they were used to help hunt woodcocks.

"hunting dogs"

"BOXERS"

BOXERS are big dogs, up to two feet high, with faces somewhat like bull-dogs. They are very gentle and intelligent, and are even used as Seeing-Eye Dogs.

Boxers have smooth coats of lovely yellow-brown, called fawn, or a sort of gray color with dark spots, called brindle. Their eyes are somewhat thoughtful, but never worried. No one knows why they are called Boxers, but it is not because they fight.

ST. BERNARDS

THIS powerful dog, with an uncanny sense of direction, was originally bred by monks in the St. Bernard region of Switzerland. St. Bernards rescue people lost in the snow drifts of the Swiss Alps. During the past 300 years, they have saved the lives of more than 2,500 persons.

COLLIES

Collies are big, shaggy dogs with long silky coats and long lean heads. Their eyes are very gentle, and they often seem to be smiling. They are often named "Laddie" or "Lassie," and everyone knows the famous film star by that name!

Collies came originally from Scotland, where they were used to tend the sheep, and they are still used more than most dogs for farm work. Yet Collies are favorite house and pet dogs. They are kind, loyal, and able to learn very difficult tricks.

GERMAN SHEPHERDS

LIKE the Collie, the German Shepherd was originally trained as a sheep dog. It is about two feet high, noble and fearless in appearance, with a rough coat any color from black to gray. German Shepherds are very loyal to their masters.

POLICE DOGS

GERMAN Shepherds are also called Police Dogs, because they can be trained to help the police track down criminals.

German Shepherds are the most loved of all dogs by the blind. As Seeing-Eye Dogs, they lead their sightless masters through crowded streets and into buses and subway trains, where no other dog is allowed.

SETTERS

THE Setter is a dog that loves the outdoors, and needs plenty of exercise. There are several kinds, and they are all known for their beauty and gentleness. The English Setter looks something like a Spaniel, and is one of the foremost of hunting dogs. The Irish Setter is always a golden red and hunts when it can, but because of its beauty it is often bred for dog shows.

DACHSHUNDS

SOMEONE described the Dachshund as half-a-dog high and a dog-and-a-half long. It is very smart and, in spite of its rather funny appearance, very brave.

Dachshunds were originally used in hunting, and one of their "faults," the slowness with which they moved, made them useful in hunting deer, because they did not frighten the animal they were tracking down. There are smooth, long-haired, and stiff-haired dogs of this breed, and they can be tan or black with tan points. Nothing is cuter than a Dachshund puppy.

CHIHUAHUAS

THESE tiny dogs weigh only between two and four pounds. Their name, pronounced "tchee-wah-wah," is that of a state in Mexico, from which they did not come; the name is just a mistake.

Chihuahuas are graceful, gay, and clever. They are also delicate, and must be protected from extremes of weather. Their small size makes them ideal house pets. Some have short hair, others are long-haired, and they come in all colors.

BULLDOGS AND MASTIFFS

PEOPLE who do not know any better take one look at a Bulldog's face, and run. This chunky dog with the wrinkled face is one of the kindest breeds, although it is hard to beat in a fight.

Bulldogs are related to another fierce-looking but gentle dog, the Mastiff, shown at the top of the next page. One of the two dogs that came to America on the Mayflower was a Mastiff (the other was a Spaniel). But while the Mastiff may be almost as big as a Great Dane, a standard Bulldog is not much taller than a Terrier.

16

"sad" "looking dogs".

MASTIFF

BOSTON TERRIERS

THE only important breed started in America is descended from the Bulldog and the Terrier. This is the neat, gay, and loving Boston Terrier. It has a slight facial resemblance to the Bulldog, but no wrinkles, and its ears are like those of a Terrier.

The Boston Terrier is most often gray or tawny with white markings on its face, legs, and chest.

17

PEKINGESE

THIS small reddish dog with the soft, thick coat has no idea of its size. It is called the "lion-dog" because its face looks somewhat like that of a lion. But it also has the courage and the pride of a lion, in spite of its size. It has a right to be proud. For more than 1,000 years, only the Emperor of China could be the master of a Pekingese.

Less than 100 years ago, the first Pekingese dogs reached England. They were taken from Peking, the capital of China, by British soldiers. Now they are favorite lapdogs, especially liked by ladies. And there is no longer any emperor in China.

POODLES

POODLES are the smartest dogs known. Most circus and show dogs are Poodles. They come in any solid color, and all (except brown ones) have black lips and noses. Their coats are curly, and they are usually clipped in what appears to be a fancy design. This custom began when Poodles were hunting dogs and their coats got in their way in the underbrush.

19

GREAT DANES

GREAT DANES are three feet tall and have short, thick coats. No other dog stands as proudly. It is one of the oldest known breeds, for its picture was painted by Egyptian artists 4,000 years ago.

DOBERMAN PINSCHERS

DOBERMANN, a German dog lover, made up his mind to breed a terrier (Pinscher in German) so that it would be the size of a shepherd dog. The dog that resulted is brave, intelligent, and obedient. It is a fine police dog and is used as a Seeing-Eye Dog.

DALMATIANS

MANY fire-houses have Dalmatians as mascots. These big white dogs, with black or brown spots, love horses and are also fine watch dogs. They are loyal, brave, and friendly, and they make wonderful pets.

21

ESKIMO DOGS

IN the cold northern regions of America live the Eskimos and their dogs, which are named after them. These dogs are not really pets. They are seldom even allowed to enter an Eskimo house, or igloo. But they are certainly helpful to everyone in the northland, because they pull the sleds hundreds of miles over the snow and ice, and can always find their way home, even when their masters are lost.

"alaskan"
dogs!

POMERANIANS

A cousin of the Eskimo Dog is the small, fluffy, gentle Pomeranian. This breed owes its popularity to one woman, Queen Victoria of England, who bought one in Florence and brought it back home.

Queen Victoria's pet weighed about 30 pounds. But the Pomeranian that is carried from home to home today weighs no more than seven pounds. This is the result of breeding, that is, of always picking the smallest puppies to be the parents of the next family.

"Fat and" Fluffy dogs!

TABBY CATS

ALL cats are soft, cuddly, and willing to purr when they are happy. They come in many colors and shapes, with long or short hair. Cats are called independent because, unlike dogs, they only love their owners when they are treated with love and understanding. But they really depend on their owners just as dogs do.

Most cats belong to no breed at all, but are mixtures of several breeds. Such cats are often striped, and are called Tabby cats. Their name comes from a kind of striped or wavy cloth called "attabi" by the Arabs.

PERSIANS AND MAINE CATS

ALL cats probably came from the East, and those with long hair are called Persians. The kittens are fluffy and will grow up with the same color—snow white, creamy white, coppery red, dusky blue, tortoise-shell (a kind of brown

24

shading to yellow in spots), charcoal gray, or jet black.

The first Persians were known as Angoras, and were a little longer than Persians are now. There are very few pure Angoras left. Some were brought to Maine a long time ago, and a new type, which some call a breed, is the Maine or Coon cat *(shown on page 28)*. It is bigger than the Persian and has a pointed tail, while other long-haired cats have bushy or kinky tails.

SIAMESE

THE best known short-haired cat is the Siamese. This breed comes from Siam (which is now called Thailand), where it is the common housecat. They are not as fluffy as the long-haired cats, and their color often changes. A white kitten may become a light-brown (fawn) or shadow-blue cat, and it will usually have darker shades of the same color on its face, legs, and tail.

The eyes of Siamese cats are almost always blue, and often they are crossed, but this does not mean that they have poor sight. All cats have very keen sight, even when the light is dim. You can see how much bigger their eyes are at dusk or by firelight. But cats cannot see in total darkness, as many people believe.

26

BURMESE

BURMA is a country near Thailand where the Siamese cats came from. Burmese cats also have short hair and long bodies, but their colors and eyes are different. Most Burmese kittens are light brown which becomes deeper as they grow. They have round eyes, colored greenish or yellowish.

MAINE

(See page 24.)

ABYSSINIAN

MALTESE

MANX, MALTESE, ABYSSINIANS

THE Abyssinian cat has fur that is more like that of a rabbit than that of other breeds of cat. It is usually brown in color, with the tips a darker shade of brown, giving the cat an interesting speckly look. It has big ears, big eyes, and is very rare.

Manx cats are different from all others, because they have no tails at all. Their hind legs are higher than their front legs, so they look like rabbits when they run. They are usually striped, either blue or brown, or solid black or white, and their heads are rather large. Real Manx cats are so rare that sometimes dishonest cat dealers cut the tails from other breeds of cat and sell them as Manx cats.

Maltese cats are beautiful blue cats of no special breed, just like Tabbies.

TAILESS

MANX

29

BIRD PETS

MANY kinds of birds can be tamed and kept in cages. There you can take good care of them. They would not be happy if they were free, like other birds, because they would not know how to take care of themselves.

TALKING BIRDS

SOME birds have voices that are almost human. By listening to human speech they can learn to talk, too. Of course, they do not know what they are saying, and they will never say anything they have not heard someone else say many times over.

Parrakeets are the most popular of talking birds. They have beautiful feathers of many bright colors, green and blue and yellow.

SINGING BIRDS

THE tame bird with the finest singing voice is the beautiful Canary, which is usually yellow. A Canary sings best when it is happy. Whistle or sing to it, and see if it does not answer.

FISHES

A PET fish is no tamer than any other fish, but it is more beautiful. Goldfish are kept in bowls where you can watch them as they dart about. At feeding time, you tap the bowl and they understand. Another pet fish is the Guppy.

CAGED PETS

Some pet animals are so small that they would get lost or hurt if they were allowed to be free, so they are kept in cages. These cages are their homes. After they know you well enough to go out for a short time, they will come back to their cages and sleep or play there.

HAMSTERS

The first Hamsters were brought here from Europe in the 1930's. These furry animals are only about six inches long. They have pointed noses and round ears and pouches in their cheeks where they store food to eat later. They love to be petted.

GUINEA PIGS

GUINEA Pigs are not pigs at all, and they do not come from the country of Guinea, but from South America where they were tamed by the Indians. They are about six inches long, with chunky bodies of various colors, pointed faces, and no tails at all. They are very gentle and talk by squeaking.

WHITE MICE

WHITE Mice are often kept as pets because they are so pretty and lively. If their cage has a tiny trapeze, such as acrobats use, they will learn to swing on it. They must always be kept in their cages.

RABBITS

SOME Rabbits are white and silky, with broad floppy ears. Others have small, perky ears and short hair. Rabbits love to be cuddled, and to play games. If they are annoyed, they show it by knocking their hind legs against the floor.

Cats may learn to play with Rabbits, but some dogs never learn this because they are trained to hunt hares, which look like Rabbits. Every Rabbit likes to have its own comfortable home which should be built like a wild Rabbit's burrow.

Domestic Animals

Longhorn
Shorthorn
Aberdeen Angus
Brahman
Holstein and Jersey
Cayuse
Bucephalus
A Knight's Horse
Percherons
Mustang and Bronco
Quarter Horse
Racing Horses
Man o' War
Justin Morgan
Comanche
Ponies
Donkeys
Mules
Sheep
Goats
Angora
Cashmere
Pigs
Chickens
Ducks
Geese
Turkeys
Fur Bearing Animals

Long before men could read or write they learned to make friends with animals. In those days all their food came from hunting or fishing. Some years there were plenty of wild animals and plenty of food. Other years animals were hard to find, and men were often hungry.

One time somebody—we do not know who—caught a pair of wild oxen, a male and a female, and instead of eating them right away, kept them until they had baby oxen. The little ones were not wild. They were saved alive until a bad year came. Meanwhile they had more baby oxen. This was the beginning of cattle raising.

Now men could live wherever they could find food for their cattle. Soon they learned to raise food for their cattle and for themselves. They became farmers.

Other wild animals were taught to live on farms. Wild sheep and goats were tamed and kept, not only to eat, but for their wool and milk.

Wild horses were taught to draw carts and both horses and oxen learned to carry heavy loads. The fierce boars of the forests became farm pigs. Large birds that lived mainly on the ground and were delicious when roasted were kept on farms and became chickens, while their swimming cousins became geese and ducks.

Those animals that could not be tamed continued to be hunted, some of them until there were no more left. Often a few were kept and put in zoos. But all over the world farm animals are kept alive to give men food or hides or wool. These animals which men have tamed are called *domestic* animals.

Buffalo

37

Longhorn

IN 1493, on Christopher Columbus' second trip to the New World, he brought with him horses, sheep, goats, pigs and cattle. None of these animals had ever before been seen in this country. Other Spanish conquerors brought more of these animals.

Massive herds of wild cattle, descended from the stock introduced by the early Spaniards, made their way to the Southwest of what is now the United States, especially to the open prairies of Texas. Anglo-Saxon settlers in this region domesticated these cattle and called them Longhorns.

Shorthorn

NEW breeds were brought to America from the farms of northern Europe. Their meat was better because they did not roam over wide prairies but were carefully fed and watched by the farmers.

The earliest and still one of the best of these breeds came from Scotland and was called the Shorthorn or Durham. The bulls provide fine beef and the cows give plenty of milk.

Aberdeen Angus and Brahman

THE very best cattle are bred to provide either beef or milk, not both.

A fine beef-producing breed is the Aberdeen-Angus, a coal-black animal that comes from the highlands of Scotland. These cattle are much smaller than the silver-gray Brahmans, which are brought all the way from India. Brahmans are usually mated to cattle of other breeds, and in this way a new breed is formed.

40

Holstein and Jersey

THE black-and-white Holstein and the brown Jersey are two of the best dairy cows. They are raised mainly for the milk they produce. The Holstein provides more milk each day, but the Jersey provides milk that is creamier.

Of course, dairy cows also produce calves. Male calves are not usually allowed to grow up. They are turned into meat, which is very tender and is called veal. Female calves are called heifers until they grow up and become cows. On farms, children often choose a pretty heifer to become a pet.

Cayuse

THE Cayuse is still seen in the West and, of course, in the movies. It is a strong, yet active animal, able to cover difficult ground at a rapid rate without getting too tired. The famous Pony Express was carried by these small horses, bringing the mail across mountains and deserts before the railroads were built. They are also called Mustangs, but the name Cayuse is most often used. Their ancestors were the wild horses of the plains. And there is no horse that brings back the memory of the Old West in the way the Cayuse does, especially when an Indian is in the saddle.

42

Bucephalus

LONG ago there was a tiny kingdom called Macedonia. The King was buying horses one day. One horse seemed so wild that the King refused to buy him. But the King's son, Prince Alexander, made friends with the black beauty, whose name was Bucephalus, and tamed him.

When Alexander became king, he conquered the world, and wherever he went he rode on Bucephalus. After Bucephalus died, Alexander built a new city and named it Bucephala.

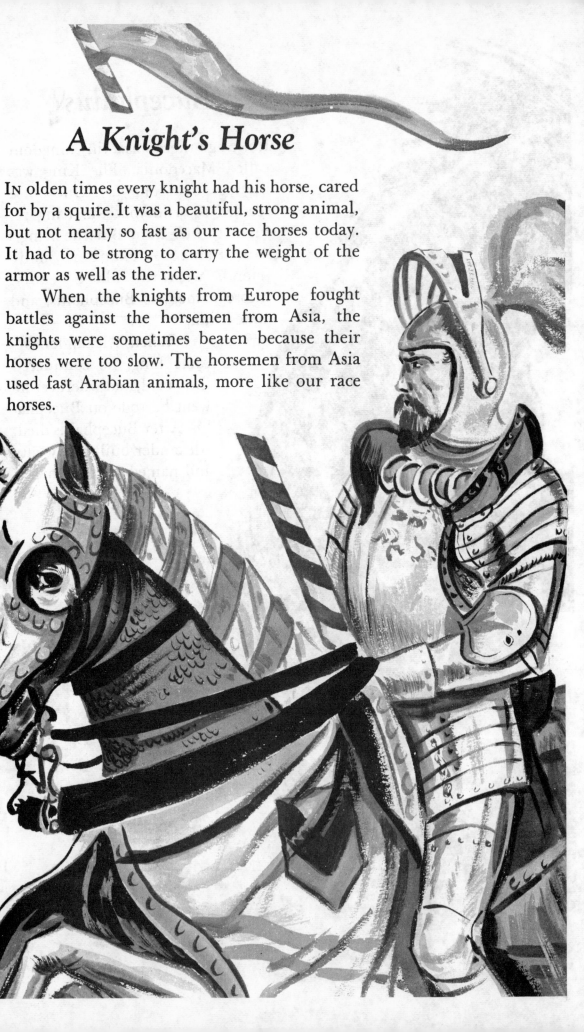

A Knight's Horse

IN olden times every knight had his horse, cared for by a squire. It was a beautiful, strong animal, but not nearly so fast as our race horses today. It had to be strong to carry the weight of the armor as well as the rider.

When the knights from Europe fought battles against the horsemen from Asia, the knights were sometimes beaten because their horses were too slow. The horsemen from Asia used fast Arabian animals, more like our race horses.

Percherons

THE Percheron is one of the most famous of work horses. It was brought here from France, and its ancestors were the sturdy horses of the knights and the lighter Arabian horses. For hundreds of years Percherons and other strong horses did heavy farm work and pulled coaches or carts. Now the Percherons are vanishing, because machines have taken their places.

45

Mustang and Bronco

HORSES first came to America with Columbus. These were called Barbs because they had originally come from the Barbary coast of Africa.

Soon there were Barbs on every ranch in Spanish Mexico. When the Indians captured many of these ranches, the horses escaped. The Barbs wandered wild all over the West for hundreds of years. When the cowboys reached the Far West they caught and tamed these horses.

The cowboys called them Mustangs. Before a Mustang is "broken" or tamed, it is often called a Bronco.

Quarter Horse

A FAVORITE breed on Western ranches is the Quarter Horse. It is usually dark in color and about five feet high. The name comes from its speed in running short distances, such as a quarter of a mile. The Quarter Horse can get in motion so fast that it can head off a steer before the creature can even begin to run off.

Racing Horses

FAST, light horses of all kinds may be called Arabian, because they come from a breed originally raised in far-off Arabia. When they first reached Africa they were known as Barbs. So many Barbs were brought to Spain that the breed was often called Spanish. These were the horses brought to America, from which the Mustang came.

One type of Arabian horse finally reached England, and is now known as the Thoroughbred. All Thoroughbreds today trace their descent from three famous animals—an Arabian named Darley, Godolphin, a Barb, and Byerly, a Turkish horse, who was used in the army before he became famous.

Thoroughbreds are fine saddle horses and racers, but for harness racing the best pacers and trotters are Standardbreds. Just as the Thoroughbreds trace back to particular Arabians, so the Standardbreds trace back to two Thoroughbreds named Messenger and Justin Morgan.

48

Man o' War

THE most popular racehorse of all time
was the chestnut Thoroughbred, Man
o' War. He was bought, when a year old,
for $5,000, but was so spirited that the
trainers could hardly control him. Then,
in two years, the horse won 20 out of 21 races
and earned $250,000 in prizes.

After Man o' War was retired from racing,
he became the father of many other great race-
horses. Horse lovers from all over traveled to
Lexington, Kentucky, just to get a glimpse of
him.

49

Justin Morgan

SOME of the most famous horses were of no special breed. One horse of this kind, who was mostly Thoroughbred, became the founder of a new breed known as Justin Morgan.

This horse, owned by a Vermont schoolteacher named Justin Morgan, soon gained the reputation of being the best horse in sprinting, pulling, trotting, or any kind of farm work. Justin Morgan, named for his master, was so popular that thousands of fine Morgan horses were descended from him.

Comanche

COMANCHE was another famous horse of no special breed. He won his fame in battle.

Comanche was one of the United States cavalry horses present at the famous Battle of Little Bighorn, which took place in 1876 and in which General Custer lost his life and the lives of his men. The victorious Indians took away the cavalry horses, as prizes of war.

But the six-year-old horse, Comanche, had hidden behind some bushes. He was badly hurt when found the next day by a party of soldiers. When he recovered the horse was received with honor. And in every parade, as long as he lived, Comanche walked behind the flags.

Ponies

PONIES are really small horses of special breeds. Shetland ponies, the most popular, are about 40 inches high. They may be black, brown, or spotted, and they have two coats, a summer coat that is short and glossy, and a shaggy winter coat that comes off in the spring.

Shetland ponies are fine pets, just big enough for a child to ride or drive. They are usually gentle, but some of them can become stubborn at times.

Donkeys

A COUSIN of the horse is the donkey, also called an ass. (If it is male, it is called a jackass.) In spite of its reputation, the donkey is not stupid. It is about the size of a pony, has short hair, and long ears.

In Mexico and South America, donkeys called burros are used to carry heavy loads.

Mules

IF a jackass is mated to a female horse (a mare), the young ones will be mules. They are hard workers, but sometimes they just refuse to work. Then they become "as stubborn as a mule."

53

Sheep

In ancient Greece, they told how a hero named Jason sailed to the end of the world to find a treasure called the Golden Fleece. This is just a story, but all over the world farmers keep shy, gentle animals, with woolly coats which can be turned into money or gold. Only tame sheep have these coats. Wild sheep, such as the Rocky Mountain Bighorns, have no wool.

The best wool sheep, Merinos, came from Spain, where the king tried to keep them. But many of them were brought out — Cortes brought some to America—and now Merinos are found all over the world. They produce very fine wool, especially a French type of Merino called the Rambouillet.

In England, they learned to breed sheep like the Lincoln which have very long wool, others like the Hampshire and Dorset which have poor wool but good meat, and still others like the Corriedale which produce wool and meat. The meat of sheep is delicious, as you know, for surely you enjoy lamb chops.

Sheep like to roam over grassland. When they have finished eating, the grass looks as though it had been freshly cut. Often more than 1,000 sheep are guarded in one flock by a herder and his dogs.

Goats

GOATS are like sheep in many ways. All goats have horns, as do many sheep, but the horns of sheep are shaped like a corkscrew, while those of goats fork up and out.

Male goats, called billy-goats, have beards. Female goats, called nanny-goats, are fine milk producers. Their milk is saved for children and sick people who cannot drink cow's milk.

Angora

GOATS have fleece, which is not called wool, but mohair. It is long and silky, and cannot mat. or felt, as wool can. The best fleece-producing goat in this country is the Angora which was first bred in Turkey.

The Angora is smaller than a sheep or a milk goat. It has long ears, horns often more than two feet long, and a noble expression.

Cashmere

FLEECE finer than that of any sheep comes from a goat found only in the valley of Kashmir, in India. Both the goat and the fleece, which is often called wool, have the name of this valley, but spelled differently—Cashmere.

Pigs

Pigs are heavy, thick-skinned animals with short legs, almost no neck at all, and a long snout. They are neither lazy nor dirty, but they do love to roll in mud, just as a dog loves to roll in grass.

Before a pig is a year old it will weigh 200 pounds. Then it is ready to be turned into tasty ham and bacon.

Some pigs are fed corn until they cannot eat any more.

They grow into hogs, weighing as much as 1,000 pounds, and they are very fat. This pleases the farmer, because all the fat on these hogs is valuable. It is turned into lard, which is used for cooking. Other parts of the animal are also useful. Strong leather is made of pigskin, and the tough hairs, called bristles, are made into brushes.

59

Chickens

In the jungles of Asia, there is a large bird with brilliant colors—red feathers on the wings, yellow on the neck and head, black on the tail. It is hard to believe that our common chicken is related to this jungle bird, but it is the same animal, except that the chicken is tame.

Almost all farmers raise some chickens, and some raise nothing else. Imagine the noise they must make, all cackling at once! Chickens provide delicious meat and billions of eggs every year.

Chickens cannot fly very high or very far. They eat by picking at their feed with their strong beaks. The little chicks are very lively.

Most American chickens are kept for both meat and eggs. The best egg chicken is the Leghorn, from Italy. If its ear lobes are white, the eggs it lays will be white too, but if the ear lobes are red, it will lay brown eggs. Both are good to eat.

A chicken farm is very noisy, because chickens make all kinds of sounds. The happiest sound comes after an egg has been laid, and the loudest comes early in the morning, when the roosters (male chickens) wake everyone with their crowing.

61

Ducks

Ducks are tame water-birds that sleep on land, but their short legs and webbed feet are not much good for walking. In the water, however, they get along fine, and as soon as they come out their feathers are dry. A mother duck gliding through the water, followed by all the little ducklings, is a pretty sight.

Farmers breed ducks for their fine meat. Long Island, in New York, is famous for its tasty ducklings. The most popular breeds are white.

Geese

A COUSIN of the duck is the goose. Its neck and legs are longer than those of a duck, but its feet are webbed and it is at home in the water.

Geese are good to eat, but the best part of all is the liver which is chopped up to make a spread. Goose feathers, which are very soft, are used for stuffing pillows.

Tame geese are gray or white. When a goose wants to talk, it makes a single loud noise, a honk, that sounds like a rusty automobile horn.

Turkeys

TURKEYS are as American as Thanksgiving, when they are almost always served for dinner. The Indians had learned to tame these big, bright-feathered birds. The Spaniards who came over after Columbus discovered America took turkeys back home, and some of them reached England. Then the Pilgrims brought a few of them back to America on the Mayflower. They must have been surprised to find wild turkeys all through the New England woods.

Turkeys, wild or tame, are beautiful birds because of their brilliant colors — green, golden, coppery in some types, although there are plain white ones too. One famous type is called the Bronze, another the Bourbon Red. They are much larger than chickens, and their meat is very solid.

You cannot be hungry after a turkey dinner. Many years ago, when families were larger, with a dozen children and sometimes more, one turkey would be just enough for a good meal. But now, few families could finish eating such a big bird, so the turkey farmers have learned to breed new types that weigh little more than a large chicken.

64

Fur-Bearing Animals

THE last animals to be raised on farms were those which are valued for their fur. Although they live in man-made homes, they never become tame, and are not pets.

The silver fox was the first animal to be kept on fur farms. Its fur is really black with hairs tipped gray or white, giving the coat a frosty look.

The mink is small, with soft brown fur. Hundreds of minks are needed to make one garment.

The chinchilla is like a squirrel, so small you can hold it in your hand. Its fur is soft and gray and thick. Chinchillas originally came from South America, but so many were killed that they became rare. Now some are raised on farms.

mink

Silver Fox

chinchilla

Wild
Animals

At one time all animals were wild. Wild animals ruled the world, many millions of years ago. As time passed, some of them became extinct, such as the various forms of dinosaurs. Others, like the dog, man learned to tame and to domesticate. Still others man hunted. Unfortunately, man hunted so well that many kinds of wild animals were on the verge of being destroyed altogether.

In recent times, man has taken many important steps to protect wild animals. Laws have been passed to regulate the number of them that can be hunted. And in almost every country in the world, there are now large zoological parks where the wild animals that once ruled the world are free to roam again and to reproduce their own kind.

68

Giraffe

THE African Giraffe is the tallest animal on land. It reaches a height of 19 feet, and its legs are so long that a man can actually stand under them.

People often wonder how this tall, unwieldy animal can protect itself from other wild animals. The Giraffe's protection comes from its hind legs. These are amazingly strong and they can give powerful, deadly kicks.

Zebra

THE Zebra is the wild horse of Africa. It is colored white with black stripes, so that it cannot be seen when it stands in the shadows of branches.

The Zebra has a large head and large ears. The short hair on its neck stands straight up. This animal can see very far, has excellent hearing, and can smell amazingly well.

Gorilla

THE Gorilla is the largest of the apes, growing to over five feet tall and weighing as much as 600 pounds. Even the lion is afraid to fight with this animal. The Gorilla will not harm people unless they attack it. It lives on fruits and vegetables.

The African mountain Gorilla is black. The jungle Gorilla is gray. A captured Gorilla becomes friendly very easily. It is smart but not as smart as the chimpanzee.

Baboon

THE Baboon, shown in the above picture on the right, is called "dog-faced," because it has a snout like a dog. The Baboon really belongs to the monkey family.

Some Baboons live in colonies or tribes, and they are ruled by the elder members. Between the various tribes of Baboons there is constant warfare.

Chimpanzee

THE African Chimpanzee is the smartest animal—next to man. It is about five feet tall and its arms hang down to its knees. It can be taught many tricks, even to roller skate.

Mongoose

THE Mongoose is a famous snake killer. Although only two feet long, it will attack a poisonous snake seven feet long. It is found in Africa and Asia, where there are many snakes. Sometimes the Mongoose gets bitten by a snake, but this does not happen often.

Aardvark

AARDVARK is a South African Dutch name which means earth pig. The Aardvark does look a little like a pig but it is not really a pig.

The Aardvark sleeps in a hole during the day. At night it comes out to look for termites. With its sharp claws, it easily tears open the termite mounds. And with its long, sticky tongue, it licks along the opened mound, gobbling up the termites.

Anteater

THE Anteater lives in swampy forests in Central and South America. The animal's long head comes to a point at the end of its mouth.

The Anteater has no teeth. Its tongue is almost two feet long, and sticky, so it can lick up ants. It uses the long powerful claws on its front feet to dig up large ant hills.

Giant Armadillo

THE Giant Armadillo lives in the jungles of South America. It has a hard protective covering over its head and body, which looks a lot like the armor that knights of the Middle Ages used to wear in battle.

Cougar

THE animal shown leaping through the air on the left side of the picture is a Cougar, or Puma. It is sometimes called a Panther. A member of the cat family, the Cougar is native to America. The Cougar can leap as many as 20 feet with ease, and 60-foot leaps have been recorded.

Jaguar

THE spotted Jaguar, shown in the lower part of the picture, is the most powerful of all the wild cats in America.

Many Jaguars live in the jungles of South America. There the owners of cattle ranches hire professional hunters to hunt the Jaguars, because these animals prey on defenseless cattle.

74

Cheetah

The Cheetah of Africa and India is one of the swiftest four-legged animals in the world. Its speed has been officially timed at 48 miles an hour, but some people claim to have seen it travel at 70 miles an hour.

Hippopotamus

HIPPOPOTAMUS is a Greek word that means river horse, but the Hippopotamus is really related to the pig. It has a very large round body and short legs. It lives in Africa, in the same waters as the crocodile, but the two animals do not bother each other. When the Hippopotamus swims, only its eyes and nose stick up out of the water.

The Hippopotamus can close its nose like a bottle cap and stay under water for as long as 30 minutes. When it comes up and opens its nose with a loud snort, a foot-high spray of water shoots out. The Hippopotamus lives on vegetables.

Rhinoceros

A VERY large, clumsy animal is the Rhinoceros. It has one and sometimes two horns on its head between the nose and eyes. This animal is very short-sighted and bad tempered. Perhaps this is why it often charges without any reason.

In India there is a belief that a Rhinoceros horn has magical powers. Some natives think that drinking from the horn will keep a person from becoming poisoned. If he is already poisoned, they think it will cure him.

Buffalo

THE Buffalo once roamed all over the North American plains. There were millions of Buffaloes in a single herd. The American Buffalo is also known as the Bison. India is the home of the Water Buffalo. The Cape Buffalo comes from Africa. The Bison is a big powerful animal. There is thick hair around its head and neck and shoulders and a black beard on its chin.

The Bison was a very important animal in the history of America. It was killed for food and clothing by the Indians and the early white settlers. Buffalo Bill was a famous hunter of Buffaloes or Bison. He was hired by the Kansas Pacific Railroad, in 1876, to kill the Buffaloes to keep them away from the railroad tracks. So many were killed that today, there are only a few thousand Buffaloes left.

Deer

DEER inhabit almost every region of the world. We speak of the adult male of most species of deer as a buck. The adult female is called a doe. The fawn is a young deer.

The antlers of male deer are those hard bones that grow from the head and look like tree branches. At the end of every mating season, these antlers fall off, but new ones grow the next year. The Moose is the largest of the deer. Caribou is the common name for our North American Reindeer. Do you remember the names of the eight Reindeer in the lovely poem, "Visit from St. Nicholas"?

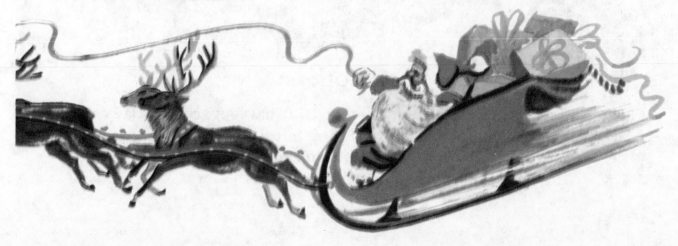

Tapir

THE timid Tapir is a strange animal. It has a massive body, short legs, and a long snout. It has five front toes but only three hind toes. The Tapir lives in Central and South America. It is a harmless animal, and is very, very shy.

Sloth

THE Sloth is the laziest of animals. It has long, curved claws which it hooks onto the branches of trees. It hangs upside down, moving slowly along a branch, while eating leaves.

80

Wart Hog

THE Wart Hog is probably the ugliest of all animals. Its head is very big and its body is small and round with pudgy legs.

The eyes of the Wart Hog squint. On each side of its face are four warts, like huge, ugly pimples. Near the end of its snout are two tusks almost a foot long. It has some whiskers on its face.

The Wart Hog is often found with zebras and antelopes on the plains of Africa.

Bear

THE Bear is a large and powerful animal, with a thick coat of hair and sharp claws. It lives in North America and Northern Asia. The Bear is a good swimmer. It sleeps all winter long. This is called hibernating.

The Polar Bear, shown above, lives in the Arctic. Its coat is white and sometimes a little yellow. It eats seals, walrus cubs, foxes and birds. It is friendly, but only when there is plenty of food around. When it is hungry it will even go after a man. The Grizzly Bear shown on the next page is even more ferocious.

The Eskimos hunt the Polar Bear for food and for clothing.

82

The Brown Bear and the American Black Bear become very timid in captivity. The Black Bear eats mostly vegetables. Honey is something every Bear likes.

Elephant

THE largest animal that lives on land is the Elephant. The African Elephant grows as tall as 12 feet and may weigh as much as 12 tons. The Elephant uses the long snout, called a trunk, to eat leaves from trees, to drink water, and to bathe itself. It also uses the trunk to scent enemies because its eyesight is very poor. The trunk is strong enough to pull up large trees.

We all know how big the Elephant's ears are. The strange thing is that the Elephant cannot hear too well. The Elephant is astonishingly smart. Once, a herd of Elephants came to a stream which was too shallow to bathe in. All the Elephants started building a dam across the stream. The dam blocked up the water and made a fine deep pool for bathing.

84

Waterbuck

THE Waterbuck on the right of this picture belongs to the antelope family. Its home is in Africa. It is really a land animal. But whenever it is frightened it hides in the water. The Waterbuck is a good swimmer.

Gazelle

THE animal in the lower part of the picture above is the Gazelle. Only the cheetah can outrun it. The deserts of Africa and Asia are the Gazelle's home.

In 1946, newspapers printed a story about a boy who was brought up by Gazelles. Natives saw the boy running with Gazelles and caught him. A doctor said the boy acted just like a Gazelle. Some people thought the boy was left by his mother and the Gazelles found him.

Gibbon

THE Gibbon ape of Asia stands only about three feet high, but its arms are so long that its fingers touch the ground. The Gibbon walks with its hands over its head and looks as if it will fall forward on its face.

In the trees this ape swings easily from branch to branch. It has a loud voice and likes to scream while eating.

Orangutan

THE Orangutan's home is in Borneo and Sumatra. It leans on its knuckles when walking because of its very long arms. A captured Orangutan ape can be taught to ride a tricycle or to put on a suit.

87

Camel

No animal is better adapted to life in the desert than the Camel. When sandstorms blow, the Camel's eyes are shielded by its very long eyelashes. We all know that the Camel can go without water for days.

Do you think that water is stored in the humps of the Camel? Actually these humps store food, not water, as most people suppose. Inside the Camel's stomach are many pouches or sacks; that is where the water is stored. Sometimes, when desert travelers have no other water supply, they will cut open these sacks and drink the water as a last resort.

Rocky Mountain Goat

THE Rocky Mountain Goat is a little like a goat and a little like an antelope. It is not really either one. It has a thick white coat with horns that curve back. It lives on high mountain peaks. It is very sure-footed and very brave.

Wild Sheep

MANY years ago, all Sheep were wild, like the Angali of Asia. These are thought to be the ancestors of all tame Sheep. They have long, curled horns. Very much like them are the wild Bighorns of our Rocky Mountains. The wild Barbary Sheep of North Africa have shorter horns that do not curl.

Lion

WE can certainly understand why the Lion has been named the King of the Beasts. The long flowing hair on its neck, called the mane, is wonderfully majestic looking. But the female Lion, or Lioness, does not have this long mane, and she does not look nearly so majestic.

Lions are the biggest members of the cat family. They sometimes weigh as much as 500 pounds. They are enormously powerful, always dangerous when they are hungry. Lions live in Africa and parts of India. They prefer the open country to the jungle.

Tiger

THE Tiger lives in regions of Asia that extend from cold Siberia all the way to hot India. There are no Tigers in Africa. The Tiger has a yellow-tan color with black stripes which hide it in the jungle. Tigers stalk their prey at night. Of all the cats, the Tiger is man's most dangerous enemy.

Leopard

THE Leopard's home is Africa. It is smaller than a lion or a tiger, but it is more ferocious. The Leopard has black spots in groups of five or six on its body. Sometimes it has so many black spots that it looks all black. The Leopard likes to stay around trees where it can hunt monkeys and birds.

Monkey

THE Monkey that lives in the jungles of Central and South America has a long tail which it uses as an extra hand when swinging through the trees. The Spider Monkey is the best acrobat. It can leap 30 feet through the air.

The Monkey of Asia and Africa does not have a tail that can grasp. This is the kind used by organ grinders and is called the Rhesus Monkey. The funniest looking Monkey lives in Borneo. It is called the Proboscis Monkey because it has a very long snout or nose, and proboscis means a long snout.

Flying Lemur

THE Flying Lemur is the size of a large squirrel. It is found from Malaya to Thailand and in Java, Burma, and the Philippine Islands. A thin, furry skin spreads from its front feet to the back feet, like sails.

The Lemur does not really fly like a bird. It spreads its feet so that the sails catch the wind, then glides through the air from the tops of trees. It only glides at night. During the day it sleeps, hanging from a branch, upside down.

Gnu

THE Gnu, or Wildebeest, of Africa, is the strangest looking member of the antelope family. It has a body like a horse and a head like a buffalo. Its horns curve down and then up, like the handlebars on a racing bicycle. There are very few of these animals left.

Antelope

THERE are many kinds of Antelopes. The Sable Antelope from the southern and eastern plains of Africa is one of the most beautiful. Its long horns curve back gracefully. The Sable Antelope's hair is short and colored black-brown and is very shiny. There are long white spots under its eyes.

The Royal Antelope is the smallest of these animals. It grows to no more than ten inches high. It lives in western Africa.

94

Gaur

THE Gaur is a wild ox. It is the largest of the wild cattle. Attempts to domesticate it have never been successful. The body is dark brown and the legs are white up to the knees.

In India and Burma, the home of the Gaur, the natives say it can pick up stones in its nose and blow them out at hunters as fast and as straight as bullets. This is only a story. The Gaur is really a very shy animal.

Wolf

THE Wolf is a form of wild dog. Some people think it is the original ancestor of all our domestic dogs. Others think it is an altogether different breed. But we do know that Wolves can be tamed, and then they become as affectionate as the most affectionate domestic dog. Since they are very powerful, they are sometimes mated with sled-dogs, to make a stronger stock.

In the wild state, Wolves can be terribly vicious and destructive. They hunt in packs and will attack sheep and cattle. They make their homes in caves and in hollow tree trunks.

Jackal

THE Jackal is a wild dog that lives in Africa and Asia. Many people call the Jackal cowardly, because it usually attacks smaller animals or animals that have been wounded by others.

Fox

Do you know the sly, clever Fox in the Aesop and "Uncle Remus" stories? The Fox is famous for its cleverness, because of the amazing tricks it will play to escape from pursuers, like running through water or along the tops of fences so as not to leave behind tell-tale tracks.

The female Fox is called a vixen. When baby Foxes or cubs are born, they stay blind for ten days, like baby kittens. And, also like kittens, cubs love to chase each other.

Coyote

COYOTE is an Indian name for the Prairie Wolf. Coyotes hunt in packs at night, uttering the most blood-curdling howls. When they hunt jack-rabbits, Coyotes work in pairs. One gives chase, while the other waits and rests, knowing full well that jack-rabbits run in circles.

97

Kaola

THE Kaola of Australia looks just like a toy bear. It has no tail. A Kaola is a marsupial. A marsupial is an animal that holds its babies in a pouch on the outside of its stomach.

Kangaroo

ANOTHER native of Australia is the Kangaroo. It stands seven feet high. With its long back legs and long powerful tail, it can jump as far as 20 feet and hop along at 25 miles an hour.

Birds

BIRDS, like people, have two legs, backbones, and warm blood. But instead of arms and hands, they have wings. They wear feathers in place of clothes. They lay eggs. The mother bird and sometimes the father bird, too, sit on the eggs to keep them warm, until the growing baby bird inside is big and strong enough to break the shell. Baby birds are almost as helpless as human babies. Their parents have to feed them and teach them how to fly.

Birds come in many sizes and in all the colors of the rainbow. The hummingbird's body is not much larger than the bowl of a tablespoon and it weighs less than the letter you drop in the mail box. But the ostrich grows eight and nine feet tall and weighs as much as two men.

The bird on this page is prehistoric. It lived many millions of years ago.

100

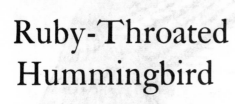

Ruby-Throated Hummingbird

THE smallest of all birds gets its name from the humming, motor-like sound of its beating wings. Like a helicopter, it can hover in one place and fly backwards. It can fly 70 miles an hour.

Whooping Crane

THE Whooping Crane is the tallest and loudest bird in North America. It is nearly five feet tall. When it whoops it can be heard all of three miles away. Usually, it lives for 50 years.

There used to be thousands upon thousands of Whooping Cranes in this country. Now there are nearly none left.

Blue Jay

FROM the tip of its beak to the tip of its tail, the Blue Jay is just a bit shorter than your 12-inch ruler. Blue Jays are very blue, very noisy, and great jokers.

On a hot summer afternoon, when owls like to sleep, several Blue Jays will gang up on a sleeping owl and awaken it with their brassy cries. Stealing acorns from squirrels is fun, too. Blue Jays gather and hide many more acorns and beechnuts than they can ever eat. But from these buried nuts forests of new trees have grown.

Strange as it seems, the beautiful Blue Jay is a cousin of the common crow. It is smaller and much more richly colored than the crow. Another Jay bird is the Robber Jay, so called because it steals food from hunters' camps.

Robin

THE Robin is the best known and best liked of all American birds. When the English settled in America they found large numbers of this member of the thrush family. They called it "Robin," because its red breast reminded them of the little English warbler called Robin they had left behind.

No American bird has adapted itself to modern civilization as well as the Robin. Today, it lives not only in villages and suburbs, but even in city parks and on the lawns of city houses. Unlike other migratory birds, it does not go all the way to South America in winter. It stops in Georgia and Florida. So the Robin is the first bird up north to hail the spring with its familiar call, "Cheer up, cheer up!"

Belted Kingfisher

Belted Kingfisher

THE Belted Kingfisher has wide stripes around the body that make it look like a barber shop pole. The males of most birds are richer or more gaudy looking than the females. The male of the Belted Kingfisher is an exception. But he makes up for it with a black crest that makes him look fierce.

The call of the Kingfisher is a harsh, rattling shriek.

Crested Flycatcher

Mockingbird

THE Mockingbird is the best singer and actor of all our birds. It will sing sweetly for hours on end, and then suddenly break off the song to imitate the song, whistle, or harsh calls of other birds.

It will imitate its cousin, the catbird, imitating a cat; and it will meow better than either of them. It will bark like a dog and has even been heard imitating the squeak of a garden gate's rusty hinge.

Mockingbird

Crested Flycatcher

THE Crested Flycatcher likes to fly after large insects and catch them in the air. It prefers to live in woodland country, but an old orchard will do. It will perch on a branch or railing for hours on end, waiting for some insect to fly by. Then it will dart quickly after the insect, snap it up, and return to its perch to wait for another insect.

The Crested Flycatcher's favorite nesting place is an empty woodpecker's hole. It will watch for a snake to shed its skin and will take the old skin to line its nest. If it cannot find any snakeskin, it will use onion skin and even man-made wax paper and cellophane. Its call is a long, loud wheeep!

Peacock

THIS most gorgeous of all birds is a native of India and Ceylon. It still lives in large numbers in the jungles of Ceylon. It has been domesticated for centuries in Europe, and struts about the lawns and gardens of the rich, and in this democratic age, in public parks, too.

The male Peacock has a train of feathers from the lower part of his back and the upper part of his tail, which he can raise and open up like a huge fan of green and blue and gold. The Peacock does this to attract the female bird who has no such fan.

Great Blue Heron

THIS long-legged water bird is a beautiful steel blue, with white markings. Its feet are not webbed like the feet of a duck and many other water birds. Its separated toes are long enough for it to curve its feet around the branch of a tree and hold on.

It builds its nests in the trees that border the swamps of Florida, Louisiana, and Texas. Sometimes as many as 100,000 of these great Herons will nest in the same place. They will return to it each year. They live on fish, frogs, snakes, shrimps, crabs, and mice. In the summer they fly north but return to the south in the fall.

Falcon

THE Peregrine Falcon, a member of the Hawk family, is also called the Duck Hawk. It is a very strong, swift flying, bluish bird with crossbars of brownish black and white spots. It has a cruel, curved beak and powerful talons. It will fly above a wild duck, pigeon, or some other smaller bird and swoop down on it, grasping it with its talons, and then will tear it to pieces with its beak.

During the Middle Ages in Europe, Falconry was a great sport of the nobles. Falcons were trained to capture certain game birds for their masters. In those days, your rank was marked by the quality of Falcon you carried about on your wrist. The sport of Falconry originated in China about 4,000 years ago.

Carrier Pigeon

PIGEONS have been serving men by carrying messages for nearly 3,000 years. Carrier Pigeons have been used mainly to carry secret messages across battlefields. Even in these days of radar, radio, and rockets, the trained Carrier Pigeons of the Army's Flying Telegraph still play an important role.

During World War II, an American Air unit had been ordered to bomb a certain Italian village believed to be held by the Germans. Minutes before the attack was to start, a U. S. Army Signal Corps Pigeon, named G.I. Joe, reached the Americans with a message saying that the town had just been taken by a British Infantry Brigade. G. I. Joe had flown the 20 miles in exactly 20 minutes! Thus he had saved 1,000 British soldiers from certain death.

Purple Martin

THE Purple Martin is the largest member of the swallow family. The male is a glossy purplish black, while the color of the female is a dull purplish black. Like all swallows, the Purple Martin has a very sweet, joyful song.

It is very friendly to people and is probably the most domesticated of all wild birds. Though it spends its winters in the jungles of the Amazon Valley, when it comes north to the United States and Canada in summer, it prefers to nest in a box-house built for it by man. Usually it will have to fight for its house with the ever-present English sparrow. Most often the Purple Martin wins. The English sparrow, by the way, is not a sparrow at all. It is a finch.

Screech Owl

You have heard the saying, "the wise old Owl." As a matter of fact, Owls are not as smart as many other birds. What makes them look like scholarly judges or school teachers is the fixed stare of their round eyes. But the Owl cannot look any other way. It cannot roll its eyes the way you can and all other birds do. It can only look straight ahead.

Baltimore Oriole

Named for Lord Baltimore, the founder of Maryland, this is the most beautiful member of the blackbird family. It has a glossy black head, neck and back. Its wings are black with a white trim, and all the rest of it is a flaming orange yellow.

It weaves its nest of grass and string, the female using her bill like a needle. The nest hangs from the tip of a high branch, swaying in the wind like a hammock, which makes a rocking cradle for the baby Orioles.

111

Starling

THE Starling is an immigrant. It used to live only in Europe, Asia and North Africa. It was first brought to New York City's Central Park, in 1890, to kill off insects that were destroying the trees. Today, there are many, many thousands of Starlings in this country.

The Starling loves company. It gathers in huge flocks that fly, without any apparent leader, in perfect and beautiful formations. It is very intelligent. It has been taught to whistle a tune and to speak a few words.

Red-Eyed Vireo

THE Red-Eyed Vireo's nest is so well built that it will last for several years. The Vireo is the victim of the lazy cowbird which sneaks its egg into the Vireo's nest. And the Vireo will sit on it, hatch, and bring up the young cowbird as if it were its own!

112

Tufted Titmouse

THE Tufted Titmouse is a perky, six-inch bird. The feathers on the top of its head stand up like the peak of an old fashioned nightcap. It does not go south in winter, but stays in swampy bottomlands.

It hunts for hidden insect eggs in the company of chickadees which belong to the Tit family, too. In summer its favorite food is caterpillars. This makes the Tufted Titmouse very popular with farmers. In winter as well as in spring and summer, the Tufted Titmouse is a loud and regular singer.

Long-Billed Marsh Wren

THIS little bird is not much larger than a hummingbird. The male usually has two or more wives. But these Wrens always build more nests than they have wives. Then, when attacked by big hawks or crows, the cagey male stands over the empty nest and chatters angrily at the attacker, while the wives sit quietly on their eggs or young ones.

113

Pelican

HERE is a well-known saying about this peculiar bird:
"There is an old bird called the Pelican
Whose bill can hold more than his belly can.
He can put in his beak
Enough food for a week
And I just don't see how well he can."

This is how the Pelican does it. Its bill is from nine to 13 inches long, and underneath the bill is a bag which is like a balloon with no air in it. This bag can be filled with food and stretched until it holds three and a half gallons! That is equal to 14 quarts of milk! The huge bill and the bag are used to scoop up water with fish in it. After making its dive, the Pelican raises its head high into the air. As the water flows out, the bag gets limp and small again and the fish slide down the Pelican's throat.

114

Flamingo

THIS vivid pink water bird is four feet tall from the tip of its bill to its toes. It breeds in the swamps of Louisiana and Florida.

The Flamingo does not build a nest in the trees or shrubs, as other birds do. But on the mud flats it builds a wide-bottomed, cup-shaped nest of clay and sticks, and lays its single egg in the center of this nest.

Sometimes, so many Flamingos build nests in the same place that they are called Flamingo cities. The birds stick their stubby, curved beaks into the mud and shallow water, and root out the shrimps and crabs they love to eat.

You might not think it, but ducks and geese are cousins of the Flamingo. The Flamingo makes a call that sounds like the deep honk-honk of many kinds of geese.

Condor

THIS is a South American vulture. It is the greatest and most powerful bird of prey in the world. It lives high in the Andes mountains of Peru and Chile. It flies higher than any mountain peaks in the United States.

The Condor never builds a nest but lays its eggs in saucer-shaped rocks. If very hungry, Condors will hunt in pairs, swooping down into the valley and carrying off a sheep, a deer, or some member of the llama family. Once plentiful, Condors to-day are very rare. Soon they will probably become extinct.

Roadrunner

ON dirt roads, from Kansas to California and south to Texas, you may see a funny-looking track with two toes pointing forward and two backward. They were made by the Roadrunner, a bird that can run as fast as a man.

It has a foot-long upright tail, long power-packed legs, and short rounded wings.

116

Bald Eagle

THE Bald Eagle is not really bald. It has white head feathers to match its white tail feathers. But its large body, its great wings, and strong legs are covered with dark brown feathers, so that from a distance it actually looks bald.

This great American bird, with its big eight-foot wing spread, lives high up on rocky cliffs. With its keen eyesight, it can watch the surface of rivers and lakes far below. From its high perch, it can swoop down upon fish, waterfowl, or upon rabbits racing for cover. With its huge, sharp talons it can scoop up these animals and carry them up to its nest.

Prothonotary Warbler

In England, many years ago, there was a kind of Chief Clerk of the courts. This man was called a Prothonotary. He wore a bright yellow hood. It seems like a big name to have given a sweet, little Warbler, just because it, too, has a golden yellow head.

Red-Headed Woodpecker

The Red-Headed Woodpecker has been called the Carpenter Bird because it spends a lot of time drilling into trees with its strong, sharp-edged bill. When you see a Woodpecker drilling into a tree, it is either making a nest or looking for insect eggs that make up its food.

Cardinal

THIS rich red, crested, black-faced bird gets its name from the color of the robes worn by a cardinal of the Roman Catholic Church. It makes its home in any area that has thickets and tangles near open spaces.

It will eat insects and fruits but its favorite foods are the seeds of sunflowers, melons, and squash. When people place such seeds where wandering Cardinals can get at them, these birds become regular residents of the locality. They repay these human favors with their rich, loud and happy singing.

119

Ostrich

THE Ostrich is the largest bird in the world. It cannot fly. But with its small wings it can run along the ground, making giant strides, at speeds of more than 50 miles an hour.

An Ostrich egg weighs three pounds and would make an omelet large enough for 14 people. The feathers on the body of the Ostrich are black but those on its tail are white. These Ostrich plumes have been prized for centuries. They used to be worn by kings and knights.

Bobwhite Quail

THE Bobwhite is the American Quail. It differs from European Quail because it does not go south in winter.

Most of the year, it is not afraid of man. It will come out on the road or visit your garden. But it *always* seems to know when the hunting season starts. Then it hides deep in woods or in tall grass. A whole flock will sleep together in a circle, with their tails pointing in and their heads out, so that they can see in all directions. People in the South call this bird a Partridge.

Whistling Swan

HAVE you ever wondered why a Swan's neck is so long and so beautifully curved? That makes it possible for the Swan to reach plants and fish at the bottom of streams and shallow ponds, without having to dive down after them.

Our native American Swan is called the Whistling Swan. But it is not the one we usually see in our parks and lakes. That is a large white Swan which is imported from Europe. All Swans make a hissing noise when they are excited. With their powerful wings, they ward off enemies.

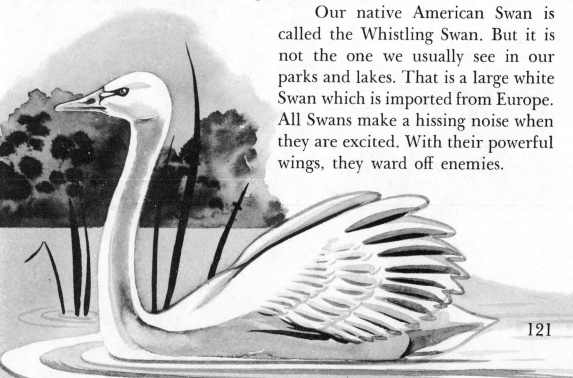

121

Egret

THE Egret is a beautiful white, long-necked bird of the heron family. It eats fish, frogs, snakes, and some water insects.

It was once commonplace up and down our coast. It was bad luck for the bird that during the breeding season, as many as 50 beautiful, long white plumes would grow out of their backs. For these *aigrettes,* as they were called, were worth 25 dollars each to adorn women's hats and heads. The birds were killed off by the thousands until hardly any were left. For many years the Audubon Society and others fought to save them. Finally, laws were passed to stop the killing. Women became ashamed to wear *aigrettes.* And so the lovely Egret lives happily again.

Mallard

THE Mallard is the common American wild duck. Wild geese are related to it. Both domestic ducks and geese were tamed from the wild varieties.

The Mallard has a broad head, a flat bill, very short legs and webbed toes. The bird is about two feet long. The upper part of the male is grayish brown and it has a chestnut-colored vest. The neck and throat are very dark green, while a thin white collar goes around its neck. The female is mostly brown, with streaks of black and buff.

Most ducks, however, are colored white, with rusty colored vests and a blue band on the wings. They all nest in the reeds along the shores of rivers and bays and other inlets of the sea. In summer they go far north and in winter as far south as Panama. There is one sort of wild duck that builds a nest which floats on the surface of the water.

123

Albatross

THE great white Albatross is not only the largest water bird, but in some ways the largest flying bird in the world. Though not as large of body as the mighty condor, its wing spread is 14 feet, which is as large as a small two-seated airplane.

The Albatross nests on high land overlooking the sea, but spends most of its time flying far out over the ocean. It can fly thousands of miles and fast enough to keep up with an ocean liner. For days it will follow a steamer. Each day when the garbage is thrown out at the stern, the Albatross will scoop up and eat whatever floats on the water. It can be tamed quite easily. For this reason, lonely sailors have grown very fond of the Albatross. They will tell you it is very bad luck to kill one.

Cormorant

THE Cormorant is a big, black bird with a white or yellow face. Cormorants live along the world's seashores.

In Chinese and Japanese waters, they have been trained to catch fish for man. A ring of hemp (of which we make rope) is tied around the bird's neck so that it is unable to swallow. Thus prevented from eating the fish, the Cormorant carries it in its bill to the boat of its owner and drops it in the boat. When the boat is full, the ring is taken off and the Cormorant is rewarded with fish for itself.

Penguin

THE Penguin lives in the far south of the world around the South Pole. It looks and acts as if it were human.

When a Penguin stands and walks erect on its stubby legs, its paddle-like wings at its sides, and with its stout body, white in front and black at the back and sides, it looks just like a short, fat man in full dress evening clothes.

Bird of Paradise

IT is truly, the Birds of Paradise, for in and around the big island of New Guinea, in the South Seas, there are more than 40 different kinds of these unbelievably beautiful birds. Not only do these birds have beautiful, rich colors on their feathery bodies, but they have extra feathers of still other colors bursting out all over them. They look like living fountains of color.

They have tails like corkscrews, movable shields of feathery color, and extra sets of wings. Their calls range from the clang of temple gongs to a harsh scream. They live on fruits and berries.

Whip-Poor-Will

THE Whip-Poor-Will is colored brownish with a few white markings. The odd thing about the Whip-Poor-Will is that nearly everyone has heard it but hardly anyone has ever seen it. That is because it sleeps all day and lives and travels by night.

It does not build a nest, like other birds, but lays its eggs on a pile of dead leaves on the ground. At night and especially before a storm, it can be heard calling on the world to "whip-poor-will," in tones so sad, that once heard you will never forget them.

Chimney Swift

THIS little bird with narrow, slightly curved wings, and not much tail, really lives up to its name. It is the fastest living thing that flies. It can go 100 miles an hour. It has been known to cover 1,000 miles in a single day.

Then, too, it likes to roost in unused chimneys. It feeds on the many small flying insects that fill the air in summertime.

128

Spoonbill

THE Spoonbill is one of the funniest looking birds. But it is also one of the most beautiful. It has a white breast, but the rest of it is a wonderful shade of rose.

It gets its name from its silly bill which looks just like a very large spoon held in its mouth, with the bowl end out. This silly looking thing is one of the most practical eating machines in Nature. With it the Spoonbill is able to scoop up shrimps and crabs and other shell fish that it cannot even see in muddy waters.

Scarlet Tanager

Most of the Tanager birds live in South America and the West Indies. A few kinds, the Scarlet Tanager among them, make the long trip up from Peru, Bolivia and Ecuador to spend their summers in the United States.

The Scarlet Tanager is the most widely known of the Tanagers. It is colored a gorgeous vivid red, and is the most brilliant of all our northern birds. You may have heard it called the "Firebird."

In our country this beautiful bird was almost killed off by men who sold its feathers to make women's hats. Laws were passed to stop this killing and one of our loveliest song birds was saved.

130

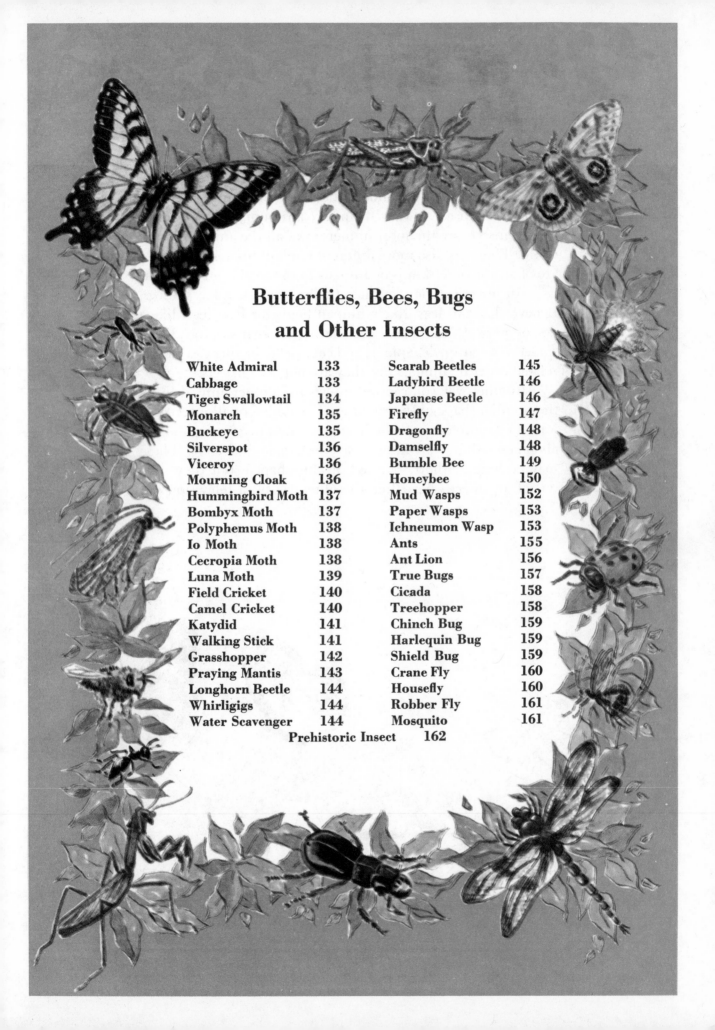

Butterflies, Bees, Bugs
and Other Insects

W E all know that butterflies, bees and bugs are insects. But have you ever wondered just what an insect *is*? Many people wonder whether or not an insect is an animal. An insect is very definitely an animal. As a matter of fact, insects are the most numerous of all the animals in the world. There are also more different kinds of insects than there are of all the other kinds of animals in the world put together.

An insect can be identified by the fact that it has six legs. It never has two legs, like a human being, or four legs, like a dog or a horse. Nor does it ever have more than six legs, like a spider or a centipede. Spiders and centipedes belong to a closely related order of animals but they are not true insects.

Another way you can tell insects from other animals is by the peculiar shape of their bodies. The bodies of all insects are joined into three parts: the head, the chest or *thorax,* and the abdomen. Almost all insects have *antennae* or feelers. These may be long or short, pointed or club-shaped, but they stick out of an insect's head like the antennae on a television set.

White Admiral

MOST butterflies like to fly about in wide open, sunny spaces. The White Admiral prefers the forest, and you will find this butterfly darting in and out of woods and along shaded paths. White Admirals are colored white, red and black.

Cabbage

CABBAGE Butterflies can be found almost anywhere, but especially where there are vegetable plants. You might think that Cabbage Butterflies like to eat a lot. The curious thing is that butterflies never eat a thing; they just sip juices. It is only when they are in the *larva* or infant caterpillar state that they eat, and then they eat a tremendous lot.

133

Tiger Swallowtail

SWALLOWTAILS are probably the handsomest of our butterflies. There is no doubt that they are the largest. You can easily spot a Swallowtail by its great size and by the tail-like parts of its hindwings. The Tiger Swallowtail has yellow wings with black stripes, like a tiger's coat.

All butterflies face the danger of being eaten alive by birds, especially when they are in the caterpillar state. Nature has a wonderful way of protecting the Swallowtail caterpillar. The front of its tiny green body has two big round yellow spots which look like the eyes of a snake. And hidden in its head are two orange horns which resemble a snake's forked tongue. These horns suddenly shoot out when the caterpillar is frightened. Birds think they have come upon a snake and are frightened away.

134

Monarch

By far the favorite American butterfly is the orange and black Monarch. Of all butterflies, this one is certainly the most accomplished traveller.

In the fall Monarchs gather in great swarms to start their famous migration to the south.

Buckeye

The Buckeye is a born fighter. This butterfly of medium size will pick a fight with larger butter-flies, and it will even pit its strength against big grass-hoppers or birds.

The upper spots on the hindwings of the Buck-eye are so large and staring that they look like the eyes of a buck deer, which is how this little scrapper got its name.

Silverspot

A GRANDER name for the Silverspot Butterfly is the "Great Spangled Fritillary." Its wings are a rich yellowish brown, the edges splashed with black, and the underwings have gorgeous spots of shining silver.

Viceroy

THE Viceroy looks just like a small Monarch Butterfly, yet it belongs to an entirely different family. This helps the Viceroy because birds have learned from experience that Monarchs have the most terrible taste. Viceroys do not have a terrible taste but because they look just like Monarchs, the birds keep away from them too.

Mourning Cloak

THE Mourning Cloak, with wings that seem to be torn at the edges, is the first butterfly to make a spring appearance.

When winter has gone, you can find Mourning Cloaks perched on bushes and tree stumps. Their chocolate brown color, with edgings of creamy yellow, make it difficult to distinguish them from the clumps of brush.

136

Hummingbird Moth

UNLIKE butterflies, moths generally prefer the darkness of night to the light of day. The Hummingbird Moth is an exception to this rule.

Though this moth often seems to stand still in midair, you would have difficulty catching one with a net. Hummingbird Moths are fast little fellows. When you start to chase after them they will dart away at speeds of up to 35 miles an hour.

Bombyx Moth

SILKWORMS are not really worms but the infant caterpillars of the Bombyx Moth. Like most moths, Bombyx lives only a few short days.

The eggs which Bombyx lays hatch into the important silk-making caterpillars. These caterpillars, spinning protective threads of silk round their cocoons, eat up a ton of leaves to make one pound of silk.

137

Polyphemus Moth

THE great Polyphemus is one of the largest of our North American moths. It is best known for the giant round "eyespots" on its hindwings. Of course, these are not real eyes but natural markings, often used by scientists to tell the moths apart. You can see why this moth is named after Polyphemus, the legendary one-eyed giant who was blinded by Ulysses.

Io Moth

THE Io Moth has "eyespots" only on its hindwings. Scientists think that Nature put these spots on the wings of some moths and butterflies to frighten away their enemies.

Cecropia Moth

HERE is the king of the moths. He is the largest moth you will find anywhere in our country. As a matter of fact, Cecropias are so large that people often mistake them for bats.

Luna Moth

IF you were asked to pick the queen of the entire insect world, could you make a better choice than this majestic moth, the beautiful Luna? The wings are gracefully curved, like the crescent of a new born moon, and when the Luna flies the tails stream behind like luxurious flowing robes.

Luna Moths lay their eggs on the twigs of walnut and hickory trees. The eggs take about two weeks to hatch into caterpillars. As fall approaches, each caterpillar curls itself up inside a leaf; there it waits to become what is known as a *pupa*. It sleeps in this peculiar state throughout the long winter. But during that time astonishing changes are taking place. By late spring or early summer, what was a caterpillar has been completely transformed into a full-grown adult moth. Then the Luna wriggles out of its pupal state and flies away to mate and to lay eggs and to start the marvelous process all over again.

Field Cricket

CRICKETS are the musicians of the insect world. Their cheerful chirps are really mating calls. Only the male crickets make music. The females find their mates by listening for the serenades of the males.

Have you ever wondered how crickets make their music? The veins on their front wings are very thick and along their hind legs are tiny ridges. The sounds come when the ridges of the hind legs are scraped against the wings, somewhat the way a violinist draws the bow along the strings of a fiddle. This insect's ears are situated, of all places, on the shins of its forelegs!

Camel Cricket

WE do not need anyone to tell us why this hump-backed insect is called the Camel Cricket. It is especially fond of damp places, and you can usually find it under the stones and logs in cellars and caves.

Katydid

When you hear the familiar "Katy did, Katy she did, she did," you can be sure it is a male Katydid singing. But he is no tattle tale, for that is all he ever says about her.

Katydids do not really sing, of course. Like all insects, they do not possess such a thing as a voice. To sing out "Katy-did," the male rubs his wings together three times; to say "she did," he rubs them twice.

Walking Stick

This insect could not be better named. It looks exactly like a stick that walks and when it is not moving you would be certain to mistake it for a stick or twig. This is one more example of Nature's marvelous way of protecting her own.

The color of the Walking Stick changes with the seasons. It is green when the leaves are green, during the spring, and when the leaves turn brown in the fall so does the color of the Walking Stick.

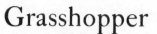

Grasshopper

GRASSHOPPERS belong to the same chirping family as crickets and katydids. They are the acrobats of the family. A blade of grass makes a fine trapeze for the Grasshopper. With its long hind legs and strong muscles it can leap far into the air. It uses its wings to glide gracefully back to the ground.

It is not easy to catch Grasshoppers. If you have ever tried you probably found that they shot "tobacco juice" at you. This "tobacco juice," which Grasshoppers spit out of their mouths, is dark brown and it has a bad smell, thus keeping the Grasshopper's enemies away.

Grasshoppers make their chirping sounds by rubbing their hind legs together. Only male Grasshoppers chirp though; and the silence of the females has led to this saying:

"Happy are the Grasshoppers' lives
They all have noiseless wives"

Praying Mantis

THIS interesting fellow usually looks as if he were kneeling to say his prayers before going to bed. That is the typical way he stands, and that of course is how he got his name of Praying Mantis. But do not let his peaceful looks fool you. He is a ferocious fighter, feared even by insects many times his size. You might call him the hobgoblin of the insect world. With his powerful front legs he can crush an enemy to death in an instant. But because he kills so many different kinds of destructive agricultural pests, he is known as the farmer's best insect friend.

You can make a wonderful pet of the Praying Mantis. You can train him to drink water out of a teaspoon and to eat chopped meat from a saucer. After every meal he will wash his face, just like a cat does with its front paws. From his corner he will follow your every move, his head cocked perkily to one side, like a playful puppy.

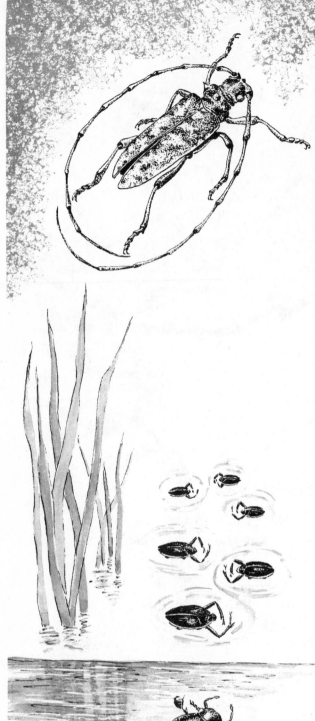

Longhorn Beetle

BEETLES have much harder shells than other insects. The shell on a beetle's back is divided into two parts which act as shields. These shields protect the beetle's delicate wings. It is only when the beetle is in flight that you can see the shields unfold.

This particular beetle is known as a Longhorn. Its antennae or feelers are amazingly long, many times the full length of its body.

Whirligigs

SOME families of beetles make their homes in pools and lakes—like these Whirligigs. They love to swim in groups.

Whirligigs get their name from the way they go whirligigging about in circles, twirling around and around, like we do when we dance the jig or polka.

Water Scavenger

THE savage Water Scavenger preys upon all forms of life that inhabit the world of pools and lakes. Unlike Whirligigs, it enjoys the land as much as the water. It is especially attracted to electric lights.

144

Scarab Beetles

THERE are many families of
Scarab Beetles. One is the well-
known "tumblebug." Its name
comes from the clumsy way it
rolls the dung of cows and
horses into round balls.

Another type of Scarab is
the Unicorn. On the top of this
page is a picture of a male Unicorn in flight. You can see from
this picture how the protective
covering of a beetle unfolds
into two shields when it is flying. Still another member of
the Scarab family is the Stag
Beetle, so called because its
jaws look something like the
antlers of a male deer or stag.

145

Ladybird Beetle

You probably know these small, spotted beetles by their nickname of "ladybugs." Did you know that they are perhaps our most valuable insects? The reason is that Ladybird Beetles love to eat mealy bugs and mealy bugs are terrible pests.

Japanese Beetle

In contrast to the helpful Ladybird, this beetle is one of our worst insect enemies.

Adult Japanese Beetles eat the foliage and fruit of a large variety of plants, while their young damage the roots by sucking the juice out of them.

Firefly

FIREFLIES are the fairy lamplighters of the insect world. They can turn their lights on and off whenever they want to, just as we would use a battery flashlight. But Fireflies do not use their lights for the same purpose we do, to see their way at night. Their lights are mating signals.

The female of this strange member of the beetle family does not have wings and she cannot fly in the air. When it is dark the female Firefly crawls up on a high blade of grass where she waits for the flashing signals of male Fireflies passing overhead. Then she blinks her own lights on and off, so that one of the males will see her signals and fly down to mate with her.

Dragonfly and Damselfly

THESE insects have the wings of airplanes and they speed through the air and swoop down upon their prey like mighty bombardiers on the attack. The Dragonfly is larger than its near relative the Damselfly. It is also a stronger flier. Dragonflies can zoom through the air at a mile a minute, making them the fastest insects known.

You may have heard the Dragonfly spoken of as "the devil's darning needle." It is also supposed to sew up the mouths of naughty children. These are superstitions, of course.

The best way to tell a Dragonfly from a Damselfly is when they are standing still. The Dragonfly always rests with its wings outstretched, whereas the Damselfly keeps its wings close together when not in flight.

Bumble Bee

THE furry bee up at the right of this page is a queen Bumble Bee. You can be sure that all the Bumble Bees you see flying about in the fall will be queens just like her. For each one you see will be the lone survivor of a large colony of Bumble Bees, and each one will be looking for some spot to spend a lonely winter.

All winter long the queen Bumble Bee will stay by herself. She will not come out of her retreat until spring, when she will start to search for a snug hole in the ground, preferably an abandoned mouse nest, which she will make into a home of her own. She will carefully line the sides of the nest with dried bits of leaves and grass. Then she will gather pollen and nectar from flowers. When at last she has stored up a sufficient quantity of food she will lay her eggs.

When these eggs have hatched and grown into a great colony of Bumble Bees, they will include a number of females or queen bees like herself. Except for these queens, the entire colony will perish when cold weather comes.

Honeybee

Is there anything more fascinating in the whole insect world than a Honeybee hive? It is a manufacturing center, a nursery, and a queen's palace.

Every hive is a community made up of thousands upon thousands of individual bees. Like people, different bees do different kinds of work, which is why Honeybees are called *social* insects. The most important member of this bee community is the great queen bee. In size she is bigger and longer than the others. She also lives longer than all the rest. Her task is to lay eggs and she performs her task amazingly well. During a queen bee's life — she lives about three years — she may lay as many as a million eggs!

Wherever the queen bee goes she is always followed by a special group of bees who feed and take care of her. These bees who form the queen's royal court are called worker bees. They even clean and comb the queen's beautiful shining coat.

In addition to the queen and the worker bees, there is a third kind called drones. They are idle, clumsy fellows who never do anything at all except mate with the queen.

Worker bees are the most numerous group of bees in any hive and it is they who do practically all the work. While some take care of the queen, others are kept busy at housework, and still others are nursemaids who tend to the hive's nursery. Each of the queen's many eggs is hatched in a separate room or *cell*. The nursemaid bees keep these cells immaculately clean, and they bathe and feed the baby bees. It is also the worker bees you see flying from flower to flower in the summer months as they gather pollen and nectar which they change into honey. A great deal of this honey is made inside the hive itself. The honey we eat is what is left over after the bees have finished feeding themselves. Fortunately for us, Honeybees make much more honey than they need.

Mud Wasps

THESE wasps make their homes of mud and clay. They have been using these building materials for millions of years, long before man got the idea of using clay bricks to make houses. The Potter Wasp builds beautifully proportioned nests of clay that look like small jugs or vases.

Mason Wasps prefer underground holes but sometimes they hang their nests from the branches of trees. And you will usually find the nests of the thin-waisted Mud Dauber Wasps in attics or barns.

Paper Wasps

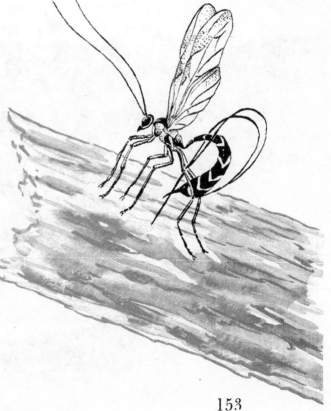

NOT all wasps build their homes of clay. Some use paper, and those that do may be truly called the world's oldest papermakers. They make the paper for their nests by chomping on bits of wood until it becomes a pasty pulp.

We have learned to make paper in much the same way, except that we use machines. Among the many families of Paper Wasps are the Yellowjackets.

Ichneumon Wasp

A CURIOUS relative of the wasp family is the Ichneumon. The female lays eggs in the strangest places. What seems to be her long curled up tail is not a tail at all but a sharply pointed hollow tube. She uses it to pierce through several inches of tree trunk to drop her eggs in places where there will be food when the eggs hatch.

153

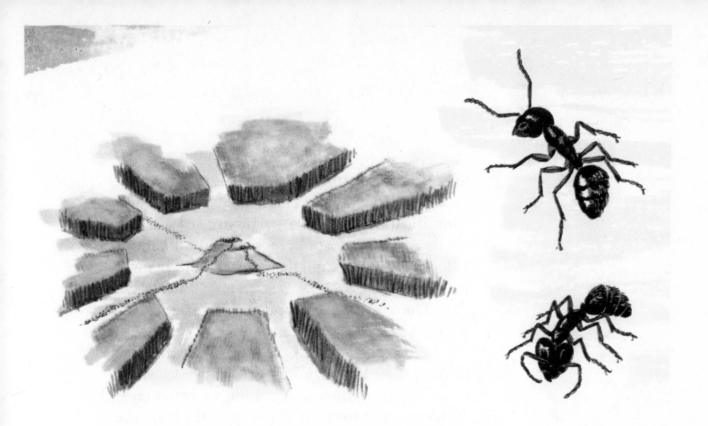

Ants

IF you have ever disturbed an ant colony, perhaps by turning over a stone under which ants were living, you may have seen them rushing about in every which way. You may have wondered about the reason for all this frantic hurrying, what it was they were carrying between their jaws, and where they were going when they suddenly disappeared into the ground.

Ants are the most highly developed of the social insects. By *social,* of course, we mean that they have developed the habit of living together, as in families or communities. Every ant community has its queen, a number of kings or males, and a great many workers. Some even have a special class of warriors or soldiers. The important thing is that each member of an ant colony has some special task to perform.

Individual ants do not work for themselves alone but for the good of their fellows. Thus, the ants you saw when you overturned the stone were probably worker ants. They were scurrying about with little *pupae* in their jaws, infant ants, which they were carrying away to safety in their underground communities.

155

Ant Lion

WE have all heard of the word "doodlebug." It has several meanings, but it is also used as the nickname for the larva of the delicate four-winged Ant Lion. Like so many insects, the young Ant Lion does not look a bit like the adult. It looks more like an ugly monster, and in a way it is.

The funnel-shaped pit on this page is the young Ant Lion's trap for some unsuspecting insect like an ant. When an ant steps over the edge of the pit it starts a miniature landslide which carries it down into the Ant Lion's waiting jaws. If the ant tries to crawl back out of the trap, the Ant Lion will shoot grains of sand at it to knock it back down again. You will find these pits near almost any ant colony. If you drop a little twig down the sides, you will see the Ant Lion hurling up grains of sand. The sand will come up like machine-gun fire.

True Bugs

MOST people make the error of speaking of all insects as bugs. Properly speaking, bugs are only a special order of insects. Therefore we should use the word "bug" only when we are referring to these particular insects and to no others.

The insects on this page are all water bugs. The Water Strider can skim along the surface of the water at amazing speeds without falling through. It uses its long middle legs as stilts and its rear legs as a rudder. Another water bug is the Back-Swimmer. The Water Boatman is similar to the Back-Swimmer, except that it paddles about right-side-up.

Cicada

THE Cicada is another true bug. It is the biggest of all the bugs. You have probably heard of the "seventeen-year locust." This is a family of Cicadas whose baby nymphs live underground for all of 17 years while they are maturing into adults.

Treehopper

THIS odd-looking fellow is a Tree-hopper, sometimes called the "Brownie" of the insect world. There are many different kinds of Treehoppers. But they are usually colored yellowish brown and green. And they all have the oddest shapes.

Chinch Bug

THE Chinch Bug is one of the farmer's worst insect enemies. Chinch Bugs are not large. They are quite tiny actually. But they reproduce rapidly and unless controlled they can destroy grain fields very quickly.

Harlequin Bug

THE gaily colored, clown-like insect on the right is the Harlequin Bug, another insect enemy of farmers. It is one of those insects popularly called "stink bugs." The odor these bugs give forth *is* horrid but it is quite harmless. Harlequins use the odor for the same reason skunks do—as a protection against enemies.

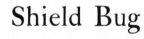

Shield Bug

THIS true bug, shaped in the form of a shield, is also a member of the "stink bug" family. The eggs of Shield Bugs are most interesting. They are beautifully ornamented, and they are always laid in clusters that look something like barrels piled in rows, one on top of the other.

159

Crane Fly

THE insects on this page and the next are all true flies. They have a single pair of wings, which is what distinguishes them from other types of flying insects. The long-legged fly on the left is the Crane Fly, often mistaken for the "daddy long-legs."

Housefly

YOU know that Houseflies are dangerous because they can carry the germs of diseases. But do you know how they carry germs?

This is how. The Housefly feeds by sucking, and so solid bits of food must always be softened before they can be digested. To do that the Housefly lets out a drop of liquid from its mouth onto the food and then sucks some of it back in. If we leave food uncovered, especially during the hot summer months when Houseflies are numerous, the food can be contaminated by these drops of liquid.

Robber Fly

THE big, hairy Robber Fly, with eyes that bulge, will pounce upon an insect flying in midair. Its legs form a basket which it uses to capture its prey while still in flight. Another name for this fly is the Assassin Fly.

Mosquito

You will never be bitten by a male Mosquito. Only female Mosquitos bite. And the only reason they ever bite is that at least once in their lifetime they must suck the blood of some warm-blooded animal before their eggs will develop properly. The larvae of Mosquitos are called "wrigglers," and they breed in ponds and pools.

Prehistoric Insect

THIS strange creature is believed to be the biggest insect that ever lived. Its wing measurements are two feet from tip to tip and the body alone is 15 inches long.

Archaeologists discovered the insect imbedded in stone where it had been preserved for millions and millions of years.

162

Fish, Shellfish and Reptiles

Plankton
Jellyfish
Crabs
Lobsters
Shrimp
Shellfish
Coral Reefs
Spawning and Migration
Mackerel
Herring
Salmon
Tuna
Black Sea Bass
Porgies
Cod
Flounder
Grass Pickerel
Catfish
Sunfish
Trout
Spotted Whip Ray
Swordfish
Sharks
Whales
Flying Fish
Porpoise
Octopus
Eels
Crocodiles
Turtles
Seals
Betta
Marlin
Four-Eyed Butterfly Fish
Clownfish
Angel Fish
Sea Horse
Sailfish

HAVE you ever stood by the edge of the sea and looked out over the endless waters that stretch way off into the horizon, and beyond? "How pretty," you must have thought as you watched the sun's rays dance merrily on this great blanket of water.

If only you were able to see through this blanket, down deep into the water, you would see sights such as you never thought existed. For just below this blanket of blue, there lives in the sea a silent world, a world of beauty, mystery, and sometimes danger.

With our new and better underwater breathing equipment, more and more of us have been able to go into this strange, silent world.

As the brave men who explore our ocean world return, they bring with them the pictures and stories of the things they have seen. As you turn the pages of this section, you will be able to share in some of the secrets and beauty of the fish, shellfish, and amphibians that live in our undersea world.

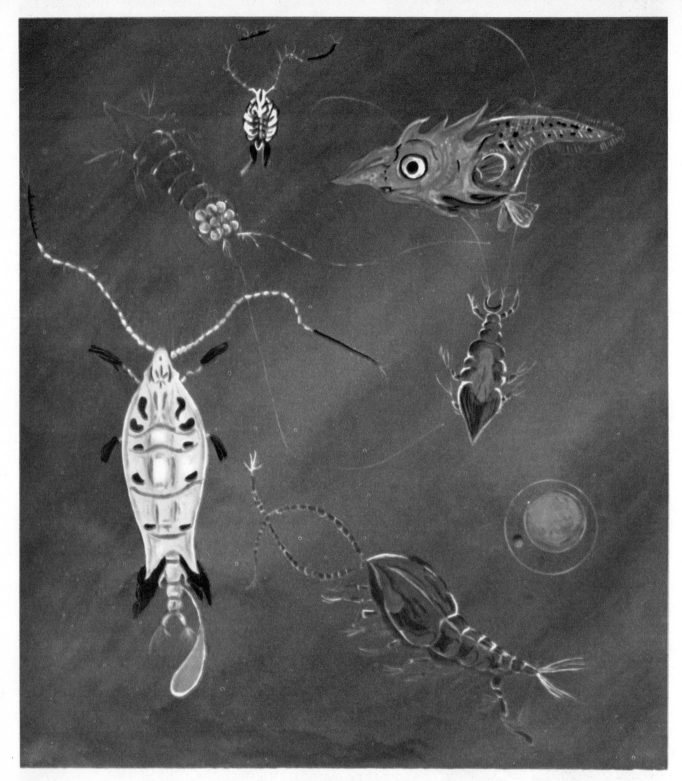

Plankton

OUR oceans are full of tiny animals called Plankton. Even though Plankton are no larger than specks of dust they are an important food for many of the fish that live in the sea.

Jellyfish

JELLYFISH are among the simplest creatures that live in the sea. There are many kinds of Jellyfish. Some of them have clear bodies that look like glass. Others have a pink or orange color. Some Jellyfish shine in the dark.

Along our shores we may find Jellyfish that are no bigger than a half dollar. In the ocean there are pink Jellyfish that grow as big as the top of a barrel. The larger Jellyfish, in the picture on this page, is a pink Jellyfish.

The smaller Jellyfish, in the picture on this page, is a Portuguese Man-of-War. The Man-of-War has tentacles that contain a deadly poison. When a fish is stung by this poison it becomes paralyzed. The Man-of-War's poison is also dangerous to man, and the slightest sting can cause great pain.

Crabs

Most Crabs make their homes in rocks and seaweed under the sea. All Crabs walk sideways, and when they grow too big for their shell, they grow a new one.

Crab-meat is good to eat. The Crab shown on the top of the page is a Market Crab. Market Crabs have much meat and are an important food for man.

Lobsters

A lobster is more like a spider than a fish. Like a spider, the Lobster walks on its many long thin legs. In the front of its body are two large claws that are used to catch and crush food.

Most of the Lobsters that we eat come from the ocean waters near Maine and lower Canada.

Shrimp

SHRIMP look like small lobsters without claws. They live near sandy beaches all over the world. Shrimp hide from their enemies by covering themselves with loose wet sand. Shrimp make tasty food.

Shellfish

ON the side of this page are popular shellfish animals. From top to bottom they are: the Snail, the Hermit Crab, the Scallop, and the Oyster. All these animals grow their own shells except the Hermit Crab.

169

Coral Reefs

IN our southern seas there are many mountains that are miles long and hundreds of feet high. These mountains are made of Coral. The Coral is a small animal that lives in the warm waters of the tropics. There are many kinds of Coral, and they all have beautiful colors.

When Coral die they leave a hard skeleton for other Coral to live on. The Coral stick together and pile on top of each other until great mountains of Coral are made. These mountains of Coral are called Coral Reefs. Some of these Coral Reefs are millions of years old.

Sometimes these Coral Reefs grow so high that their tops stick out of the water and become small islands. Coral Reefs can be dangerous to man. If a ship crashes into a hidden reef it may be wrecked.

Under the sea many fish make their homes in the small caves that are found in Coral Reefs. Wherever there is Coral many fish and plenty of food can always be found.

172

Spawning and Migration

THE seasons change, and summer turns into winter. In the sea, fish can no longer find food and shelter. The sea becomes cold and empty. The fish must move. Unless they find food and shelter they will die.

Millions of fish gather together with their families. They are ready to begin their long yearly journey. This journey is called *Migration*.

Somewhere along the way, or sometimes at the end of their travels, the fish find a safe place for the females to place their eggs. When fish lay and hatch eggs, we say they are *Spawning*.

After the eggs are hatched the fish continue their trip. Soon millions of fish appear in our bays and along our beaches. Fishermen have been waiting for them with lines and nets. Thousands of fish are taken from the sea. Some fish are put into cans for food, and other fish are sent fresh from the sea to the markets.

Fish are good to eat. They are full of vitamins and minerals, which help make us big and strong.

173

Mackerel

ONE of the strongest food fish found in the sea is the Mackerel. Even though it is not much bigger than the herring, it has great strength and speed. It swims in groups that stretch as long as 20 miles. The Mackerel never seems to stop to rest but is always moving.

The Mackerel is always hungry and it will eat plankton, other small fish, or herring.

Every spring many Mackerel come to the waters of the North Atlantic Ocean to find food, and a place to drop their eggs. They have no one favorite spawning ground, and they will put their eggs wherever it is safe for the eggs to hatch.

At the top of this page there is a picture of an Atlantic Mackerel. Another kind of Mackerel is the Spanish Mackerel. This fish makes its home in our southern seas.

The Atlantic Mackerel is found in the North Atlantic Ocean along the American and European coasts. The Atlantic Mackerel usually grows to about 12 to 16 inches long, and weighs from one to three pounds.

The Mackerel is a very important food fish and is sold in stores in both North and South America, and Europe.

174

Herring

OF all the fish that live in the sea, the one that is most important to man is the Herring.

The Herring is a small fish that never grows much more than 12 inches long. Herring swim together in large groups called schools and each school may have a million or more fish in it. There are so many Herring in our oceans that we cannot even guess at their number.

Every year many Herring die. Thousands are caught by fishermen, and many more of these fish are attacked and eaten by bigger fish.

Strange as it seems, in spite of all these dangers the number of Herring in the sea never gets smaller. One reason for this is that each female Herring may have up to 30,000 babies a year, and for every male Herring there are three females. Another reason may be that Herring always have plenty of food. They eat plankton and only have to open their mouths to strain in plankton from the sea water whenever they are hungry.

Fished for by man and eaten by the other fish in the sea, the little Herring feeds the world and somehow is still the most plentiful fish found in the sea.

Salmon

PACIFIC Salmon are born in fresh water lakes and streams. The young fish swim to the Pacific Ocean where they stay until they have grown into strong adults. Then they return to the inland lakes and streams. To get there, they must fight upstream against strong rapids and jump over large rocks and waterfalls.

Tuna

Tuna are big, strong fish. They grow as long as ten feet and may weigh up to 1,000 pounds. They swim through the water at very high speeds and always fight very hard whenever they are attacked.

One of the favorite members of the Tuna family is the Bluefin Tuna. These fish swim in large schools and are found in the warm waters of the Atlantic and Pacific Oceans.

Fishermen catch Tuna with nets, harpoons, or strong fishing poles. Most of the Tuna's meat is put into cans and sent all over the world for us to eat.

Black Sea Bass

THE Black Sea Bass makes its home on rocky or rough bottoms and near old shipwrecks. Most large Bass are found near the shores of New York and New Jersey. Sea Bass usually weigh about two to five pounds and are very good to eat.

Porgies

THE Porgy is a popular food fish found in the Atlantic Ocean along our northeastern shores. They grow to about nine inches long, and live on the bottom of the ocean where they feed on small fish and worms.

Cod

THE Codfish is one of the most important food fish in the world. These fish are found in the cold waters of the North Atlantic Ocean. The Codfish weighs from ten to 35 pounds. There are always many Cod in the sea. One Codfish can lay as many as four million eggs!

Flounder

To most people the Flounder may seem to be a very ordinary fish, but this is far from the truth. When the young Flounder begins life it swims upright, like all other fish. As this strange flat fish becomes an adult it turns and swims on its side. The young Flounder has eyes on each side of its body. As the Flounder grows, one eye begins to move upward, so that it can see properly as it swims on its side.

Flounder rest on the bottom of the ocean. Their undersides are almost colorless, but their top sides can change color to blend with the ocean bottom. Their color may be anything from a sandy tone to shades of dark brown.

There are winter and summer Flounder. Winter Flounder live in shallow cold water in the North Atlantic Ocean. Summer Flounder prefer warmer waters and many of them are found during the summer months along the New York shores.

Grass Pickerel

GRASS Pickerel live in lakes and quiet streams. They like to make their homes in shallow water where there are weeds and a muddy bottom.

The Grass Pickerel is a small fish and often people mistake it for a baby northern pike.

As a sport or game fish, the Grass Pickerel is not very important because of its small size.

Catfish

CATFISH are among the most popular fish in America. There are many different kinds of Catfish living in our fresh water lakes and streams.

Most Catfish like warm muddy waters. They will eat almost anything that they find on the muddy bottom.

All Catfish have small eyes and long feelers that look like a cat's whiskers. Unlike most other fish, Catfish have no scales.

Catfish are very hardy and can live out of water longer than most fish. Many people like to eat Catfish.

180

Sunfish

THE little Sunfish is one of the most popular fresh water fish in the United States. There are many different kinds of Sunfish living in our streams and lakes. Most of these fish are only three to eight inches long. Sunfish have bright blue, yellow, and orange colored skins.

These fish are always plentiful and are easy to catch on a small hook baited with a worm. Even though they are small they make a tasty meal.

Trout

SPORTSMEN have fished for Trout since the days when America was first settled.

Most Trout live in cool, rushing streams. They eat insects, worms, and other small fish.

Spotted Whip Ray

THE giant Spotted Whip Ray lives in the warm waters of our southern seas. It looks like a bat and swims by flapping its great wings. The Whip Ray grows as large as 20 feet wide and sometimes weighs as much as 2,000 pounds.

Even though these fish are big and strong, they have no teeth and are not dangerous unless they are attacked by man or other fish.

Swordfish

A SWORDFISH is as big and as strong as a shark. It has a long bone in front, that looks like a sword, which it uses to kill other fish.

Sharks

SHARKS are feared by men and fish. But most Sharks will not attack fish or man unless they are sure they will win.

The most dangerous Sharks are the big man-eating White Sharks. These Sharks attack anything, and fear nothing.

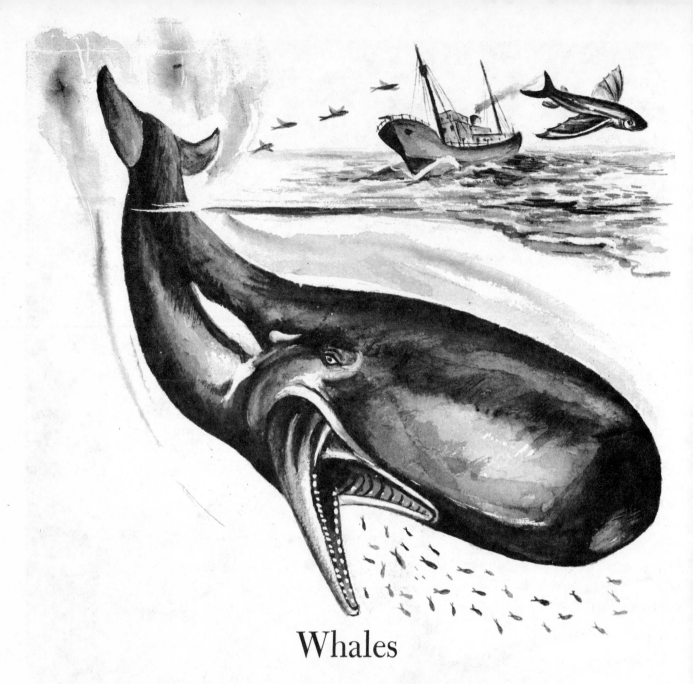

Whales

WHALES, the largest animals in the world, spend all their lives in the water, like fish, but they really are not fish. Whales are mammals. A mammal is an animal that has hair and warm blood. All mammals take care of their children. Dogs, cats and cows are mammals that live on land. Can you think of others?

Unlike fish, Whales must breathe air, and cannot stay under the water for more than 20 or 30 minutes.

Sperm Whales, like the one you see in the picture above, are valuable for the oil they carry in the top of their heads. Man uses this oil to make soap and perfume.

Flying Fish

THE Flying Fish does not really fly, but it can glide hundreds of feet through the air. This small fish, although never more than 12 inches long, has very large fins that look like wings. When the fish jumps out of the water it spreads its fins and glides over the waves like a bird.

Porpoise

PORPOISE are mammals like the whales. Porpoise always swim in large schools. They can swim very fast and they often jump out of the water high into the air. Porpoise have sharp teeth which they use to fight sharks.

Porpoise are very smart and can be taught to do many tricks. They are friendly animals who love to have fun and to show off.

Octopus

THE Octopus is an ugly monster that lives among the rocks on the bottom of the sea. It has eight strong arms and a mouth that looks like a parrot's beak. When an Octopus is attacked, it will wrap its arms around its enemy and pull it to the bottom of the sea.

Eels

EVEN though the Eel looks like a snake it is a true fish. All Eels are born far out at sea. They swim thousands of miles until they reach inland streams. When the Eel is ready to spawn it returns to the sea where it was born.

Crocodiles

CROCODILES are amphibious reptiles that can live on land and in water. Crocodiles are found in tropical countries all over the world. They like to make their homes near sluggish rivers or open swamps.

Crocodiles have webbed feet which help them walk easily on soft wet ground. Crocodiles feed on small animals and fish, which they swallow whole. Sometimes a Crocodile will attack a large animal or even a man.

Crocodiles lay eggs. They bury their eggs under sand or in nests of weeds and plants. The female Crocodile guards the nest until she can hear her babies grunt. Then she digs the babies out of the nest.

Crocodiles are important to man. They have a tough skin which is made into leather for shoes, handbags, and traveling bags. We make perfume from the oil in their glands.

187

Turtles

THE Sea Turtle is born on land but its life is spent in the sea. When the mother Sea Turtle is ready to lay her eggs she leaves the sea and climbs onto some sandy beach. On the beach she finds a safe place away from the water, and digs a hole in the sand. After burying her eggs in the sand the mother Turtle, who is now very tired, slowly crawls back into the sea. She will never see her children. Soon the eggs hatch and the baby Turtles go down to the sea where they will spend the rest of their lives.

On the top of this page is a picture of a Hawksbill Turtle. The shell of this Turtle is used to make beautiful tortoise-shell combs and jewelry.

The picture just above is that of the Green Turtle. This Turtle can grow to be over four feet long and weigh more than 500 pounds. This big Turtle is used to make Turtle soup.

Seals

THE Seal is an air-breathing mammal. Even though the Seal spends part of its time on land, its real home is the sea. There the Seal is a graceful animal, but on land it is clumsy and awkward. Whenever there is danger the Seal rushes to the safety of the sea.

In the picture below, on the left, is a Sea Lion. Sea Lions are the smartest members of the Seal family. Most of the performing circus Seals are Sea Lions.

The Sea Elephant on the right is the largest member of the Seal family.

Betta

THE Betta is a small, tropical, fresh-water fish that is never longer than three inches.

Whenever two male Bettas meet there is a great battle, and they fight to kill. When fighting with a male, or breeding with a female, the male Betta spreads his fins like an ostrich and shows off his beautiful colors. Because of their great beauty, these small fighting fish are bred and kept in aquariums by people all over the world.

Marlin

STRIPED Marlin are found only in the Pacific Ocean. They are huge fish that weigh 600 pounds or more.

It is thrilling to see this fish streak through the water at top speed and then leap high into the air. The Marlin is famous as a game fish because of the great fight it puts up when it is caught on a fisherman's hook.

Four-Eyed Butterfly Fish

THIS little fish lives in the waters of the West Indies. It is a very colorful fish and very popular among tropical fish lovers all over the world. This fish got its name because of the large black spot that it has on each side of its back fin. The spot looks like another eye.

Clownfish

ONE of the greatest enemies of small fish is the sea anemone. The sea anemone looks like a flower, but it has long, waving tentacles that are full of poison.

For some strange reason, the sea anemone does not harm the Clownfish. Whenever this funny looking fish is threatened by danger, it swims in among the anemone's tentacles where other fish are afraid to follow.

Angel Fish

THE Angel Fish is one of the most colorful fish found near coral reefs.

It has a flat, brightly striped body that shines in the water as it swims lazily along.

This fish is called an Angel Fish not only for its beauty, but because its fins look like wings.

192

Sea Horse

THE Sea Horse is a strange looking creature. It is a true fish, but it swims in an upright position and has no tail fin.

Like all other fish, it breathes through gills which are on both sides of its head. Its body is covered by tiny scales that join together to make a hard suit of armor.

One of the strangest things about the Sea Horse is that the father has the babies instead of the mother. The father has a pouch like a kangaroo. The mother puts her eggs in this pouch and then goes on her way, leaving the father to hatch the eggs. When the eggs are hatched, about 200 baby Sea Horses swim out of the father's body.

Most Sea Horses are only three or four inches long. They are found along the shores of most tropical seas.

Sailfish

SAILFISHING is an exciting sport enjoyed by many people. The Sailfish lives in the Atlantic and Pacific Oceans. When it is caught on a fisherman's hook, it will leap high out of the water and fight ferociously to get the hook loose.

The Sailfish is not very good to eat because its meat is very oily. Fishermen like to stuff and display this beautiful fish in their homes.

Flowers and Plants

Garden Flowers
Iris
Rose
Lady-Slipper
Crocus
Lily-of-the-Valley
Lily
Pansy
Bleeding-Heart
Dahlia
Sweet Pea
Camellia
Carnation
Bachelor's Button
Peony
Gardenia
Hibiscus
Amaryllis
Zinnia
Daffodil
    Tulip
    Hyacinth
    Gladiolus
    Poppy
    Aster

Chrysanthemum
Rhododendron
Clematis
Violet
Wild Flowers
Bluebell
Goldenrod
Buttercup
Dutchman's Breeches
Honeysuckle
Venus's-Flytrap
Ferns
Carnivorous Flowers
Foxglove
Pitcher Plant
Desert Flowers
Hedgehog Cactus
Saguaro or Giant
    Cactus
Useful Plants

Cotton
Peanut
Peppermint
Parasitic Plants
Orchid

Every living thing is either animal or plant. Plants can grow up into the air or down into the ground. They cannot go from place to place as animals do. Animals have to move to hunt for food. Plants make the food they need out of sunshine, air, and minerals from the soil.

With a wonderful chemical called chlorophyll, which makes their leaves green, plants manufacture sugar. This sugar is the source of

196

all the food in the world. For animals eat plants
or other animals which have eaten plants. So it
all goes back to the sugar in the plants.

Trees, shrubs, grasses, vines, and weeds are
all plants. Like all living things, plants can reproduce their kind. The flowers make this possible. Just as animals are male or female, so flowers
are *staminate* and *pistulate*. The stamens hold
the pollen. Deep within the pistils are the ovules
or seeds of life.

Nature makes flowers beautiful, gives them
a lovely smell, and fills them with honey-sweet
nectar so that they will lure the insects. When
butterflies, bees, and hummingbirds go from
flower to flower gathering nectar, they carry pollen to the seeds. These unite in the miracle of
creation.

Garden Flowers

GARDEN flowers are those that we plant, water, weed, fertilize and otherwise take care of ourselves. This is called cultivation. All of our cultivated flowers were once wild flowers.

Flowers we replant each year are called annuals. Perennials are those that will bloom year after year.

Iris

IRIS is so hardy that it will survive the cold of Siberia and also the heat of India. Iris is the Greek word for rainbow, and it comes in all the colors of the rainbow. Blue Flag, a wild Iris, grows in meadows in this country. Iris is the state flower of Tennessee.

Rose

THE most beautiful and best known of our garden flowers is the Rose. There are wild Roses in many of the cooler parts of the world. They have been cultivated for many hundreds of years in China, Persia, and Europe. Cultivated Roses are like domestic cats and dogs. People have cross-bred different kinds of Roses to make new and more beautiful kinds.

The most beautiful of all Roses, the American Beauty Rose, was really an accident. One day some years ago, it appeared in the corner of a garden in Washington, D. C. The bees had mixed up the pollen and seeds of Roses that would have been kept strictly apart if the garden had not been neglected.

199

Lady-Slipper

THE Lady-Slipper, a cousin of the orchid, gets its name because one part of it is shaped like a lady's slipper.

There is a smaller kind that hides away in deeply shaded bogs. It is called the Fairy Slipper. Another, which the Indians called Moccasin Flower, can be replanted and grown in your garden.

Crocus

LIKE the robin, the Crocus tells us that spring is on the way. This tough, little flower pushes up through late snow.

Sometimes it is so white it cannot be seen. But it grows in your favorite colors too. From the orange-streaked flowers of one kind of Crocus comes the coloring used on candy and cakes.

200

Lily-of-the-Valley

THE Lily-of-the-Valley is a dainty, little member of the lily family. Its blossoms look like nodding, small, white bells. It has a lovely, sweet scent. It grows wild in the woods of Europe and northern Asia. In the United States, it grows in the woods of our eastern mountains.

Lily

THE Lily is a very large family of flowering plants. It includes not only Lilies and lilies-of-the-valley, but also such flowers shown on other pages as iris, hyacinth, tulip, and daffodil. And believe it or not, asparagus, leek, onion and garlic are in the same family as Lilies.

Pansy

PANSY is from the French *pen-sée* which means thought or remembrance. Pansies have funny little clown faces made by darker markings on light ones.

Bleeding-Heart

THIS pretty flower has heart-shaped, deep pink blossoms and fern-like leaves. You will find the Bleeding-Heart in many gardens.

Dahlia

THE original Dahlia was a small red flower with a yellow center.

Sweet Pea

THE Sweet Pea comes in more different colors than any other flower.

Camellia

THE Camellia Japonica is the beautiful blossom of an evergreen shrub closely related to the tea plant. In the south it is called just Japonica.

Carnation

THE Carnation is probably the most popular flower after the rose. The Red Carnation is the state flower of Ohio. Related pink Carnations grow wild.

Bachelor's Button

IT is said that an unmarried man wears this flower to find out if his girl loves him.

Peony

PEONIES are native to eastern Asia and southern Europe.

State flower

203

Gardenia

THE Gardenia has very shiny, deep green leaves. The flower is a waxy-looking white, a creamy yellow, and it has been produced in a pinkish white.

The Gardenia is native to the hot parts of Asia and Africa.

Hibiscus

THIS is the name of a large, showy, bell-shaped flower. It is sometimes seven inches wide and may grow on a stem seven feet tall. It may be white, rose, or pink.

Hibiscus is also the name of a very large group of related plants. One kind is the tall, graceful Hollyhock and the Althea or Rose of Sharon.

Amaryllis

AMARYLLIS is the name of a whole family of beautiful flowers. It comes from a Greek word meaning to sparkle or twinkle. Amaryllis have bulbous roots and look like lilies.

Zinnia

THE Zinnia was once an ugly, little flower that no one wanted. But cultivation has made it into a beautiful garden flower. It now comes in different shades of scarlet, rose, orange, yellow, purple, and red. There are double-flowering Zinnias and a little pompom that blooms for weeks. The Zinnia is the state flower of Indiana.

205

Daffodil

DAFFODILS and the related jonquil look alike, but you can tell them apart because the jonquil has no leaves on its stem. Both flowers grow from bulbs planted in the fall. They blossom in April.

Tulip

HOLLAND cultivates Tulips of every solid color and combination of colors, and sends millions of Tulip bulbs to the rest of the world. Now we grow Tulips too, especially in the state of Michigan.

207

Hyacinth

THE small blossoms come in blue, purple, lilac, pink, red, or white. They are closely packed in bell-shaped clusters.

When Hyacinths were brought to America in colonial days, a wild Hyacinth grew here. It was so prized by the Indians that when white men trampled a field of them, it started an Indian war.

208

Gladiolus

THE purple, red, orange, yellow, or white blossoms of the Gladiolus grow on only one side of its long stem facing the sun. The bulbs have to be stored away from frost in warm cellars each fall and replanted in the garden when spring comes.

Poppy

THE Poppy is native to many different lands and climates. The beautiful, golden-yellow Poppy is the state flower of California. The oriental Poppy of Turkey and Armenia is a flaming red with a purple-black center.

209

Aster

ASTERS are among the commonest of wild flowers. There are also many different garden varieties. Most of the wild Asters are blue, lavender, or pinkish. All these have yellow centers. The cultivated Chinese Asters have no yellow center. There is a giant California Aster which grows three feet tall.

210

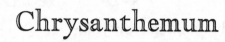

Chrysanthemum

THE Chinese cultivated the Chrysanthemum more than 2,500 years ago. The Japanese made it their national flower.

Today we raise it in red, purple, yellow, and white. It comes in dainty, little button-hole flowers and in huge eight-inch soft balls on stems four feet long.

Rhododendron

THE Rhododendron is an evergreen shrub or tree. Sometimes it is only six feet high, but some kinds are 15 and 20 feet high. It has showy, shiny, deep green leaves.

The big flowers are from three to six inches across. They may be lilac-purple, pink, or white. They grow wild in the mountain woods of Virginia and south to Georgia. They also grow on the Pacific coast. The Rhododendron is the state flower of Washington.

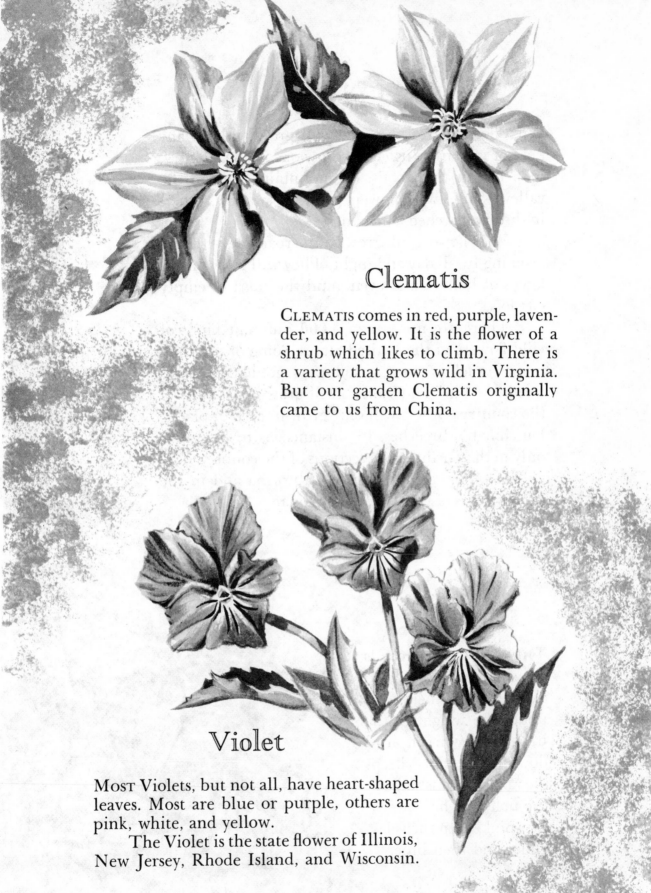

Clematis

CLEMATIS comes in red, purple, lavender, and yellow. It is the flower of a shrub which likes to climb. There is a variety that grows wild in Virginia. But our garden Clematis originally came to us from China.

Violet

MOST Violets, but not all, have heart-shaped leaves. Most are blue or purple, others are pink, white, and yellow.

The Violet is the state flower of Illinois, New Jersey, Rhode Island, and Wisconsin.

Wild Flowers

WILD flowers are those that will grow without any help or care from us. They grow out in the country, in fields, in the woods, on mountains, and in the valleys. Some wild flowers grow in swamps, others in the dry, parched land of deserts.

Wild flowers will grow by the roadside with cars zooming by all day and night. They will grow on the lawns of houses, and even amid the trash of empty city lots.

There are more than 3,000 different kinds of wild flowers in the United States. Some of the commonest, such as asters, cornflowers, goldenrod, milkweeds, orchids, and violets, will grow in all parts of the country. Others will only grow in certain places. Dutchman's breeches, for instance, is to be found only in the northeastern sections of the country. The golden poppy grows only in California and in the nearby parts of Nevada and Arizona.

Bluebell

THE stems of Bluebells are straight from one to two feet high, then bend under the weight of the blossoms which nod downward. This keeps the rain from washing out the pollen. The flower is first pink, then turns lavender and then blue.

214

Goldenrod

GOLDENROD is the state
flower of Alabama, Ken-
tucky, and Nebraska.
There are more than 100
kinds of this bright yel-
low flower in the United
States. They grow in all
parts of the country.

Buttercup

THIS little flower looks like a cup and is the color of butter. It has large, green leaves forked like crow's feet and is sometimes called Crow's Feet, too.

There are 40 different kinds of Buttercup in the United States. The giant Buttercup grown in gardens is from China and is called Trollius.

Dutchman's Breeches

THESE white blossoms with yellow centers are shaped like a heart and have feathery, fern-like leaves, but they *do* look like little Dutch boy's pants hanging on a line upside down.

These flowers grow wild from Canada to South Carolina and westward to the Great Plains. They are closely related to the bleeding-heart which came to us all the way from China.

Honeysuckle

THE small, trumpet-shaped Honeysuckle flowers are red outside and deep yellow inside. The lovely trumpets give out no sound, but a heavenly, sweet smell.

Honeysuckle may be either a shrub or a woody climber. This kind will twine its way through the woods or over a porch trellis.

217

Venus's-Flytrap

THE Venus's-Flytrap is a carnivorous
plant and grows in the south. It has two
trap leaves, one on each side of the
flower. These leaves are four inches long.

On the inside surfaces of the leaves are tiny trigger hairs.
When an insect steps on two of these hairs, the leaf starts to
fold. In less than one second it has snapped shut with the insect
locked inside. It takes the leaf a day to digest a small insect, but
a week for a big one.

218

Carnivorous Flowers

CARNIVOROUS means flesh or meat eating. So a carnivorous plant is a plant that eats flesh or meat. This sounds rather strange when we recall that plants are living things that manufacture their own food. Well, these carnivorous plants are nature's exception.

Carnivorous plants are unable to get enough nitrogen from the soil as other plants do. So they have to get nitrogen in the same way you do, by eating things that contain it. But as these plants cannot move to go hunting, they trap insects in strange ways to get their steaks and chops.

There are two such carnivorous plants shown in this book. One, the Venus's-Flytrap, is on page 218. You will find the other, the Pitcher Plant, on page 221.

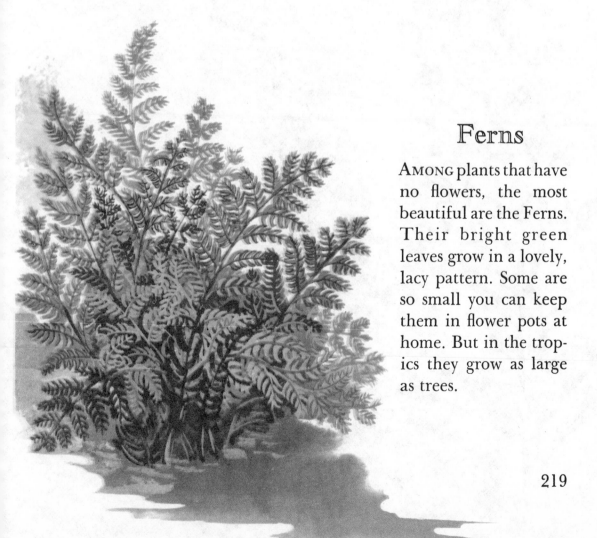

Ferns

AMONG plants that have no flowers, the most beautiful are the Ferns. Their bright green leaves grow in a lovely, lacy pattern. Some are so small you can keep them in flower pots at home. But in the tropics they grow as large as trees.

219

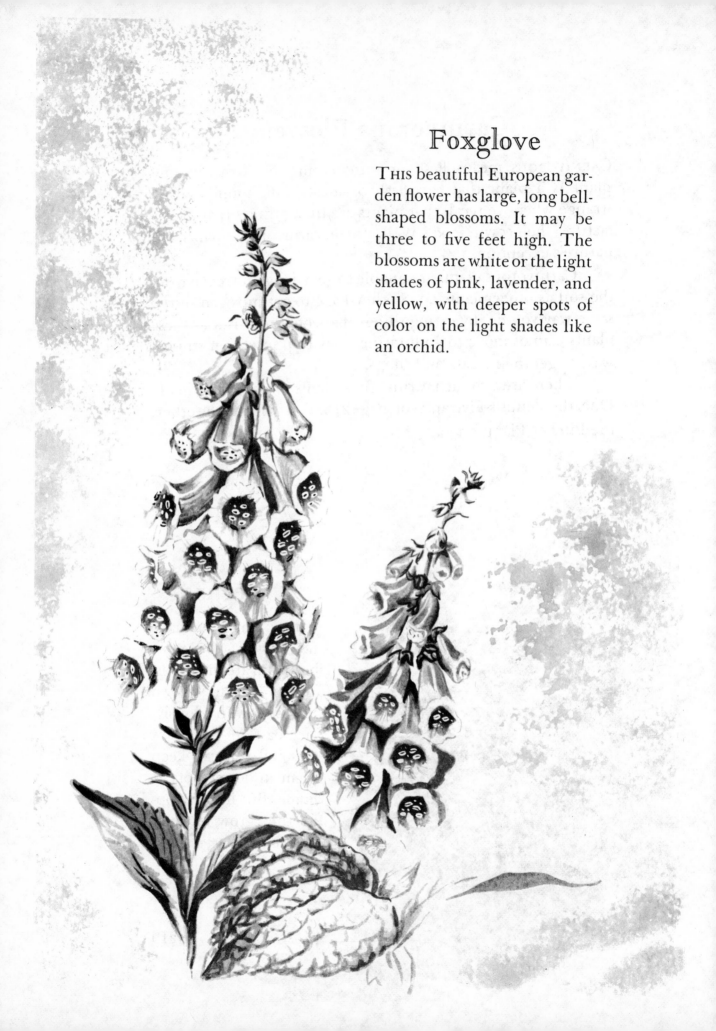

Foxglove

THIS beautiful European garden flower has large, long bell-shaped blossoms. It may be three to five feet high. The blossoms are white or the light shades of pink, lavender, and yellow, with deeper spots of color on the light shades like an orchid.

Pitcher Plant

THE odd plant shown here is another carnivorous plant, just like the Venus's-Flytrap. Here is how this plant gets its nitrogen: Its tall flower is shaped like a tall pitcher. And just like a pitcher it can hold water.

A spider, fly, mosquito, or other insect landing on the slippery lip of the Pitcher flower, slips down into the rain water that has collected. Then the flower digests it.

221

Desert Flowers

AFTER one rain the desert turns into a carpet of flowers. But they bloom for only a day or two. Typical are the belly plant flowers. They are so small and close to the ground that you have to lie on your belly to see them. Just as typical is the 40-foot tall cactus.

Hedgehog Cactus

THE Hedgehog Cactus shown on this page is a native of the higher land in Arizona. It is one of the few cacti whose flowers last more than a day. Its beautiful red-wine colored, shiny flower lasts five days. Its purple fruit is delicious to eat.

Saguaro or Giant Cactus

THE flower of the tree on the right is colored a creamy, waxy white with a large, bright yellow center. It is the state flower of Arizona. The Cactus has roots that are able to absorb huge quantities of water, which are sucked up into its stalk and branches.

222

Useful Plants

THERE are many flowering plants that are good for more than the beauty of their blossoms. There are herbs that give us peppermint for candy and dill for pickles. There are the plants that give us peanuts, cotton and many other useful things.

Cotton

THE white blossom of the Cotton plant blooms for one day. It leaves a pod called a boll on the end of the stalk, which bursts open a few weeks later. Then the Cotton is ready to pick for the manufacture of thread and cloth.

Peanut

THE Peanut is not a nut at all. It is a tiny vegetable in a pod like a pea. When the pod starts to form, the stem of the Peanut plant turns downward and pushes the pod underground, where it matures so the plant will grow out of the ground again.

224

Peppermint

THIS three-foot high plant is a herb and a member of the mint family. It has a small, pale blue flower. Its oval, shiny leaves are toothed and pointed. They give an oil used to flavor chewing gum, candy and ice cream. In medicine this oil is used to help relieve indigestion, toothache, and, in menthol inhalers, for hay fever and colds. It is also used in ointments to help headache. Michigan produces one half of the world's supply.

Parasitic Plants

PARASITES are plants which attach themselves to other plants and draw food from them. Mistletoe is a typical parasite. The tropical orchid also attaches itself to the bark of trees. But it does not take food from them. It sends its roots into the air from which it gets nourishment.

Orchid

THERE are 10,000 different kinds or species of Orchids. No other plant in the world has so many different species. The most beautiful Orchids are the kinds that are grown in greenhouses and in the tropics.

226

Trees and Shrubs

Birch	Palm
Maple	Cypress
Ash	Poplar
Chestnut	Sycamore
Elm	Mulberry
Butternut	Eucalyptus
Beech	Fig
Balsam Fir	Rubber
Hemlock	Hickory
Pecan	Basswood
Persimmon	Black Walnut
Magnolia	Teak
Sassafras	Mahogany
Cedar	Cacao
Oak	Huckleberry
Redwood	Cottonwood
Spruce	Willow
Pine	Azalea
Apple	Privet
Cherry	Hydrangea
Dogwood	Forsythia
Lilac	

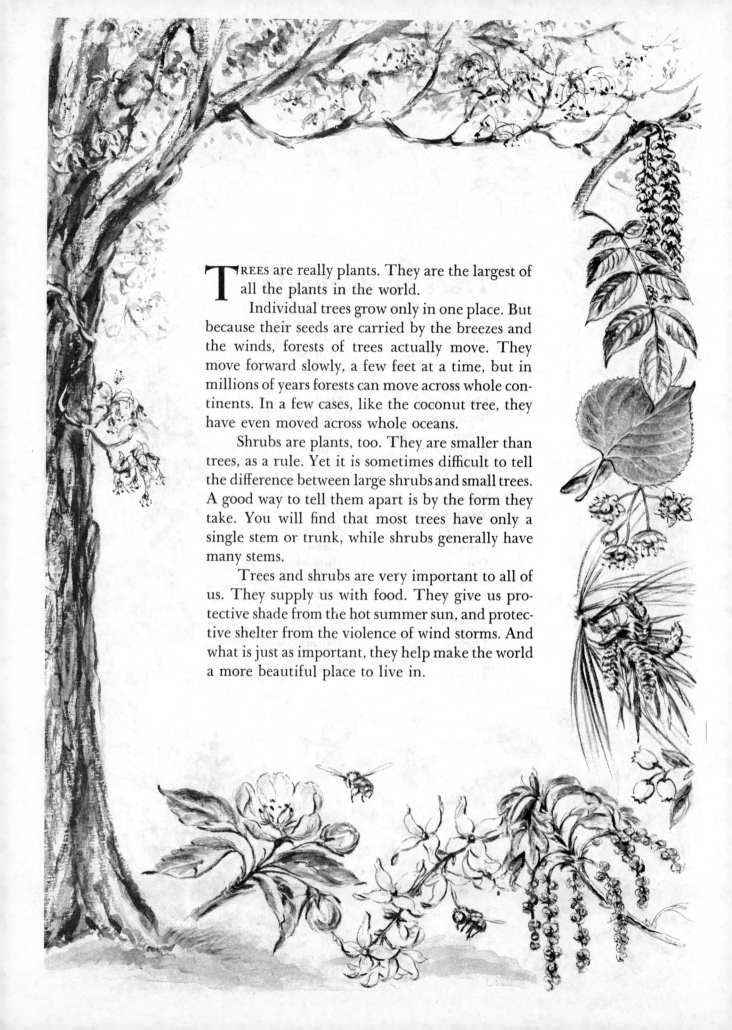

Trees are really plants. They are the largest of all the plants in the world.

Individual trees grow only in one place. But because their seeds are carried by the breezes and the winds, forests of trees actually move. They move forward slowly, a few feet at a time, but in millions of years forests can move across whole continents. In a few cases, like the coconut tree, they have even moved across whole oceans.

Shrubs are plants, too. They are smaller than trees, as a rule. Yet it is sometimes difficult to tell the difference between large shrubs and small trees. A good way to tell them apart is by the form they take. You will find that most trees have only a single stem or trunk, while shrubs generally have many stems.

Trees and shrubs are very important to all of us. They supply us with food. They give us protective shade from the hot summer sun, and protective shelter from the violence of wind storms. And what is just as important, they help make the world a more beautiful place to live in.

Birch

IF you have seen a Birch tree, you know how slender and graceful it is. A variety of Birch tree is called the Paper Birch because the bark, when peeled off, can be used to write on. The outside bark is white and marked with lovely charcoal-colored streaks.

The Indians made canoes from the bark of Birch trees, because it is waterproof. The bark of the Sweet Birch is dark brown, with lots of short white lines. From the Sweet Birch comes wintergreen oil.

229

Maple

THE Sugar Maple has a sweet sap
which is used to make maple syrup.
But this tree has other uses, too. The
wood is used for furniture and also
for fuel. In the spring there are yellow-
green blossoms on the branches of the
Maple. Each seed possesses a wing.
There are always two seeds joined
together so the two wings can be
carried by the wind. And from these
winged seeds new Maples grow.

The Sugar Maple is but one of
about 115 different varieties of Maple.
Other popular members of this tree
family are the Norway, Oregon, Silver,
Moosewood and Japanese Maple.

Ash

STRANGE as it seems, the Ash is a member of the olive tree family.

In the old myths of the Scandinavian peoples, the Ash held a very important place. They believed that the world was supported by a mighty Ash tree, and that it was from an Ash tree that the first man was formed, while the first woman was formed from an Elm tree.

Chestnut

SOME time ago, the Chestnut trees of our Appalachian woods were nearly all killed by a bark disease. Today, young twigs are growing out of the old trunks. Perhaps they will be able to grow into fine trees again. Most of us know how good the nuts are to eat.

231

Elm

THE American Elm looks like a bursting sky rocket. The trunk splits into branches which grow up and away from the main trunk and then curve suddenly down towards the ground.

Many Elm trees are planted in New England towns along both sides of a street, and the high branches overhang to form a beautiful archway.

232

Butternut

THE leaves of the Butternut tree are light green early in the summer. During the summer they slowly turn yellow. The Butternut tree is found in northern North America all the way west to the Rocky Mountains.

The Butternut is not a strong tree and does not live long. But it does have a delicious tasting nut about one to two inches long. The nut is very pasty, sticking to the branches after the leaves have fallen off.

Beech

THE Beech is a fine shade tree, because its spreading branches have so many thin leaves. The wood is hard and is used for fuel and for lumber. It belongs to the same tree family which includes the chestnuts and the mighty oaks.

In the winter, the trunk of the tree is smooth and gray. In the autumn, nuts fall to the ground from hard, thorny shells. The meat in the nut is very sweet.

233

Balsam Fir

MOST of our Christmas trees are Balsam Firs. They are a popular choice, because the needles do not fall off quickly and because they have a pleasant pine scent. Unlike the spruce, whose cones grow down, the cones of the Fir grow up.

It belongs to a large group of trees called evergreens. They are called evergreens because they stay green all year round.

234

merry christmas!

Hemlock

THE Hemlock is the best known evergreen in North America. In the forest, it grows as high as 100 feet. The wood makes excellent lumber. The leaves of this tree are delicate, short and flat. The top of the leaf is bright green. The bottom of the leaf is light green and silvery.

The flowers of the Hemlock blossom in the spring. They turn into small cones, colored red-brown. They do not fall off the tree until the next spring.

Pecan

THE Pecan tree belongs to and is the largest member of the hickory family. Some Pecan trees grow as high as 150 feet. They have very big trunks. The Pecan nut is shaped like a very tiny football that has a thin shell which can be cracked easily to get to the very tasty nut meat.

Persimmon

THE playful possum loves to sleep in the branches of the Persimmon tree. He eats the fruit and then goes to sleep hanging by his tail. The Persimmon is an odd looking tree. The trunk is straight, but the bark is cracked into small pieces, and the branches curve out from the top in the funniest shapes.

The fruit of the Persimmon looks like a small yellow apple. It is wonderful to eat, but only when it is ripe. Persimmon wood is very hard and is used to make the wooden heads of golf clubs. Persimmon trees grow best in the southern part of the United States.

Magnolia

THE southern Magnolia tree has so many leaves that it is hard to see the trunk. The flower of this beautiful tree is the state flower of Louisiana.

The rich green leaves have the texture of leather. The Magnolia has lovely sweet-smelling white flowers that bloom in the spring.

Cedar

THE nice-smelling wood used to make cedar closets and cedar chests comes from the Red Cedar tree. The wood is very hard and it has a light red color. The fruit of the Red Cedar is a small blue berry.

There is also a northern White Cedar whose fruit is a cone. When it is ripe, the cone peels open like a banana.

The southern White Cedar has cones which split open from the center.

Sassafras

THE Sassafras tree is most unusual. Each branch has three leaves of different shapes but evenly colored a beautiful green. Most Sassafras trees are small and slender. But some grow up to 100 feet tall. In the fall the leaves turn to a gorgeous scarlet.

There is a big caterpillar that makes its home in the Sassafras tree. It turns green when it eats the green leaves. This caterpillar becomes the beautiful swallowtail butterfly. Sassafras tea is made from the roots of the tree. The dried and powdered leaves are also used to flavor Creole gumbo soup.

238

Oak

You may have heard the saying, "From tiny acorns mighty Oak trees grow." These acorns are the nut-like fruit of the Oak trees, and they contain the seeds which grow into new Oak trees. Roasted acorns are good to eat.

There are two main kinds of Oak: the Black Oak and the White Oak. The White Oak is a majestic looking tree. The great strength of its wood makes it excellent for building ships and furniture. The bark of the Black Oak is very dark and its wood is not so strong as the wood of the White Oak.

Redwood

REDWOOD trees are the oldest and the tallest of all living things. A Redwood can grow as tall as 350 feet and as wide as 22 feet. Some of these giant trees have holes cut in them so that cars can drive right through.

A sister to the Redwood is the still wider Big tree. These trees grow to an unbelievably old age, and many are more than 2,500 years old!

Spruce

THE Spruce is another evergreen tree. The leaves of the White Spruce are colored a whitish-green. There are many of these trees along the coast of Maine. The White Spruce is one of the favorite Christmas trees.

There is a Norway Spruce which is wonderfully suited for building tall masts and spars on sailing vessels. Most of the wood used for paper-making comes from Spruce trees.

Pine

THE Pine is still another variety of evergreen tree that keeps its needle-like leaves all year long. There is an easy way to tell Pines from other evergreen trees. The needles of the Pine grow in peculiar small bunches of two to five each. The Sugar Pine of California and Oregon is the tallest of the many kinds of Pine trees.

Apple

THE Apple tree has a short, thick gray trunk that is twisted like a piece of clay. In the spring white, sweet-smelling flowers bloom from the tree. But the apples do not ripen until fall. The twigs on the branches that hold the apples are short and thick. They cannot sway in the wind, so the apples are not damaged by knocking together.

No one knows why, but if you plant a seed from one of our sweet apples, such as the McIntosh, the new tree will grow small apples that have a sour taste. That is why new Apple trees are grown from twigs and not from seeds.

242

Cherry

BLACK Cherry trees have dark red buds, long leaves and bark that turns black with age. The cherries that come from this tree are not colored black, as you would imagine, but purple. The early American settlers prized the Cherry tree very highly. They used its strong wood to make beautiful cabinets and furniture.

Dogwood

ONE of the most beautiful flowering trees is the Dogwood. In New England the flowers are pure white. They bloom early in spring before most of the other trees. The Dogwood is not a tall tree, and the white flowers blooming next to the dark trunks of taller trees make a particularly lovely sight.

Palm

THE Palm is a tropical tree. In the United States it only grows in the southern parts of California and Florida. The trunk of the Palm does not get thinner towards the top, as do most North American trees. It grows straight, like a wide pole with a bulge at the very bottom. There are no branches on the Palm tree, but great leaves grow out of the tree top.

A common Palm tree in California is the Canary Island Date Palm. The orange-colored date fruit hang down in bunches.

The coconut of the Coconut Palm is the biggest seed in the world. The white liquid inside it is called coconut milk and it is very nourishing. On some tropical islands the coconut makes up an important part of the native diet. The coconut looks something like a monkey's face.

Cypress

THE Cypress is a sad, gloomy looking tree, which is probably why many ancient civilizations used it at funerals and as a symbol for mourners.

The Bald Cypress, which grows in swamps in the southern part of the United States, is an especially strange tree. The bottom of the trunk has ridges like a half-opened umbrella. Part of the roots stick up out of the water all around the tree and look like bent knees. No one knows exactly why they stick up. But they are ideal for making the curved bottoms of wooden boats. Cypress wood is also used to make railroad ties.

Poplar

THE Poplar is easy to recognize. It grows straight up and is very narrow. The branches grow out from the trunk only a little before they curve almost straight up.

In parts of Europe, the people grow long rows of Poplars along the highways and rivers, because they act as effective windbreakers.

Sycamore

THE Sycamore is sometimes called the Buttonwood or Buttonhole tree. In the winter, the tree's fruit look like little balls hanging from strings on the upper branches. The Sycamore is the oldest hardwood tree on earth. The branches grow at different angles. While the bottom of the trunk is always white, the upper bark is colored beautiful shades of white, gray and purple.

246

Mulberry

You will often find the White Mulberry in old New England towns. The trunk of this tree is short and it has a wonderful way of leaning to one side. It is a good shade tree. The fruit ripen a few at a time all summer long rather than all at once like the fruit of most trees. People do not like to eat mulberries but birds love them.

The Mulberry is the tree silkworms live on. If you cut a twig when the sun is hot, you will see the white sap which the silkworm uses to make silk.

George Washington had many Mulberry trees brought to the United States. He had hoped to start an American silk industry, but the early settlers found that it was not a profitable venture in this country. Today, most of our silk comes from Japan and India.

247

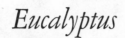

Eucalyptus

THE Eucalyptus tree is grown in California as a windbreaker. It grows high above the houses, and the trunk of the tree usually slants to one side. The leaves are long and thin and are colored blue-green. They hang in bunches. When the sun is hot the leaves roll up and turn their edges to the sun so they will not be dried up. Eucalyptus oil is made from crushing these leaves.

Fig

THE Fig tree has been the main source of food in regions around the Mediterranean Sea for thousands of years. The figs it gives are very plentiful. That is because of the astonishing fact that instead of bearing fruit only once a year, like most fruit trees, the Fig tree gives two crops every year.

Today, Fig trees are grown in the United States, too, especially in California and Texas.

Rubber

THE Rubber tree grows only in tropical climates. The tree is tall and thin. The bark is smooth and light colored. The flowers are green with yellow centers.

It is the juice of this tree that is used to make rubber. The juice, which is between the outer bark and the inner wood, is white and looks like thick milk. That is why it is called latex. Latex comes from a Latin word which means milk. Workers tap the Rubber tree for this latex by cutting narrow grooves in the bark. They slant the grooves downward. Then they place a cup at the bottom of the tree, and the latex drips into it.

249

Hickory Nuts

Hickory

HICKORY wood is hard and heavy and is used to make tool handles, like axes. Hickory wood is also burned to smoke meats, like hickory-smoked bacon. The bark looks shaggy. That is why the Hickory is also called the Shagbark tree.

The Hickory grows best along water banks and on hill-sides through most of the eastern half of the United States. The meat inside the Hickory nut is very delicious. Another Hickory is called the Bitternut because its nuts have a bitter taste.

250

Basswood

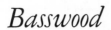

In the summer, groups of yellow flowers shaped like stars cover the Basswood or Linden tree. The flowers have a very strong smell. Bees love them.

The wood from the Basswood is used to make toy airplanes and Venetian blinds.

Black Walnut

The Black Walnut has many light green leaves that look very pretty next to the dark bark. These lovely leaves fall off at the end of the summer before the leaves of any other tree. The nut of this tree has a most unusual flavor and is used in ice cream and cakes.

251

Teak

THE Teak tree grows in southern Asia and in great numbers in Burma. The wood is used for ship building, especially for decks. It is also used for fine furniture. Teak wood lasts a long time. Houses built of this wood have lasted for hundreds of years.

During the rainy season, small white flowers appear at the tips of the branches of the Teak tree. These trees may grow as high as 150 feet and as wide as 15 feet, but they take 100 years to reach that size.

Mahogany

MAHOGANY is one of the most popular woods. Today most Mahogany wood comes from Central America. The wood comes in different shades of brown, polishes easily, and is very strong. It is used to make furniture, musical instruments and expensive boats. Some Mahogany trees are grown in southern parts of Florida and California for decoration.

Cacao

WHEN Columbus came to the West Indies and Central America, he found the Indians drinking something they called chocolate. It was made by grinding and roasting the seeds of the Cacao, a beautiful evergreen with leaves that are reddish on the back. The seeds, as big as almonds, are in a brown pod. This is the fruit of the Cacao tree. We have changed its name to cocoa and use it not only to drink, but to make candy and cake.

Huckleberry

THE Huckleberry shrub is found throughout North America and Europe. The leaves have yellow scales on the undersides. The berry fruit is blue or sometimes black. It has always been considered good to eat, especially in pies.

Blueberries are better tasting, though, and now that more blueberries are being grown, the Huckleberry may become less popular.

254

Cottonwood

THE eastern Cottonwood is a member of the poplar tree family, and it grows east of the Rocky Mountains. It is a fast-growing tree, reaching a height of 100 feet.

Like most fast-growing trees, the Cottonwood is not strong. The branches are easily broken by storms. The triangular leaves have a saw-tooth edge.

Willow

WEEPING Willow is one of the few trees mentioned in the Bible, that is still living. The Weeping Willow, shown on the left, is tall and straight. The branches are thin and hang down. The tree looks as if it were weeping.

The Pussy Willow, shown on the right, is in the same family as the Weeping Willow. In early spring, catkins, which are like small balls of cotton on the branches, are a common sight.

Azalea

THE Azalea is one of the most lovely garden shrubs in the world. It comes in many colors, and it would be difficult to imagine a new home in the temperate or northern parts of the United States, where the Azalea grows best, that does not have one of these lovely shrubs in its garden.

Privet

A VERY popular garden hedge is made with the Privet shrub, because it grows straight and is easily trimmed. The Privet will grow rapidly in almost any soil and grows very well in the northern states. The leaf is smooth and green. There are small black berries which do not taste good, but birds like them.

256

Hydrangea

HYDRANGEA shrubs have beautiful clusters of pink, white, or blue flowers. They bloom along sea shores where it is not too cold. The French Hydrangea is a large round bush and has very shiny leaves. The Oak-leaf Hydrangea grows around New York City. There is a Climbing Hydrangea, shown below, which climbs up walls and trees and has large white flowers in June.

Lilac

THERE are at least 500 different kinds of Lilac shrubs. In the spring the flowers are very colorful. The common Lilac is the oldest shrub planted in American gardens. It is also the state flower of New Hampshire.

The most popular Lilacs used to be the purple and white bushes. Today, people like some of the other kinds better, like the Korean Lilac. It has pink flowers and blooms earlier than most of the others.

Forsythia

THE Forsythia shrub is also known as the Golden Bell. The flowers bloom early in spring and the leaves stay green until late fall. One kind of Forsythia, called the Ovata, was brought to the United States from Korea. It has yellowish flowers which bloom before any of the other Forsythias.

There is a new kind of Forsythia called Spring Glory. The many large yellow flowers should make it very popular.

258

Animals! (chart)

ANiMAls ARe

OUt -OF- SiGht.